Having Your Cake
and
Eating It Too!

The Hedonist's Guide To Opulent, Decadent and Orgasmic Living!

Margaret Braunack

ACCESS
CONSCIOUSNESS®
PUBLISHING

Having Your Cake and Eating It Too!
Copyright © 2014 Margaret Braunack
ISBN: 978-1-939261-71-7

Published by
Access Consciousness Publishing, LLC
www.accessconsciousnesspublishing.com

Printed in the United States of America

Contents

Acknowledgments

I would like to dedicate this book, to all of the people who have contributed to my life. To my amazing children, you are the gifts that demand of me that I continue to choose more of me. To my family and friends and those who have empowered me and continue to do so I am so grateful and lucky to have you in my life. Thank you to the people that I have met along the way; for showing up to allow me to see more of me.

My deepest gratitude to two of my friends Petra Hunting and Lilian Cunningham who got the energy of what I was choosing to create with this book, and inspired me with the title and sub-title.

I would like to acknowledge Gary M Douglas, the Founder of Access Consciousness®, for the gift that he is in facilitating change on our beautiful planet. His awareness and generosity of spirit has been a massive contribution to my life and my living and he continues to show me the "what else is possible?" I am so grateful.

This book would not be in existence without this amazing man and his awareness and contribution.

Dr Dain Heer, thank you for your immense kindness and for always being the invitation to me especially when it gets tough. You are truly being "Be You and Change the World!"

Your Invitation

As you get the vision of a beautiful mouth-watering cupcake that sits so neatly and contained in the frilly decorative cupcake paper case, and is so perfectly iced and decorated: would you be willing to ponder this possibility?

Are you living your life as the cupcake in its entirety? Delicious yummy moist cake with tastebud tingling icing and wrapping yourself in a warm decadent case that is nurturing and caring for you?

Or are you seeing you and your life as dry stale cake, with unappetizing icing and an inedible cupcake case that protects you from the hurts and pain that are dished out?

What if this was a metaphor for your life and living? Which scenario are you choosing?

What are you creating as your life? Are you ready to have your cake and eat it too? Are you ready for the real you to start showing up?

Is it time to see you as the gorgeous, delicious and moist you with the depth of a luscious chocolate mud cake? Would you be willing to remove the protective case and to have total vulnerability: for this is where your strength lies? For you and others to see, eat and enjoy the cake you first must remove the case, regardless of how decorative and frilly it is. Or are you only willing to see the cake case and think that's all there is?

Is this enough for you? Are you happy being convinced that the decorative paper case is all that there is to you and your life? What if the real deal is what is inside that paper case, you being you, regardless of what anyone else thinks about you?

Are you aware that it takes approximately four seconds for people to form an opinion or judgement of you from your first meeting? What are they really judging? Can they really see you or only your cake case? Is this all that we have been taught to look at?

What if we never again had to prove our worth, or even to impress others? What if unwrapping you and discarding the case isn't that terrifying? What if it is totally ok to be different? What if you never had to destroy you again trying to fit into a world that doesn't work for you?

What are you using to keep yourself from having your cake and eating it too?

CHAPTER ONE

Where It All Began!

I have had snippets of my life having some clue of what it was like to "Have my cake and eat it too," and much of my life not so much, as I had been so entrained to get my life right by this reality's standards and to fit in to what everyone else was choosing. It was all about being the same as everyone else and hiding my difference. This all started to change for me around the age of twenty-two, for this is when I really started to become aware that there was so much more available and all I had to do was choose differently. The snippets were no longer enough for me. It was time to break the mould of what I had grown up with, and of course this didn't often endear me to others. It was the first time that I started to realise that the people around me didn't want me to choose differently and be different. This is where the "Just for me, just for fun, never tell anyone" concept came into existence for me. I didn't talk to people a lot about what I was choosing as I knew that their judgements of me and my choices would kick in. A real taste for life and living came alive in me that I hadn't even known existed before. I started to find and do things that brought me joy. Drinking great champagne and eating delicious food, wearing beautiful jewellery that brought me joy. Making my clothes with beautiful fabrics and enjoying and laughing until I was ready to burst with some amazing friends.

Walking in the rain and drinking Pina Coladas by the pool at some relaxing resort. I would be lying if I said that it was all roses because it wasn't. There were many good, bad and ugly times and now I can honestly say that I am so grateful for it all, for every choice that I have made has made me into the person that I am today, someone who has a demand for so much more possibility and awareness.

Having lived in the "either or" universe for a long time, I now know that making different choices and being willing to continually add to my life is what truly allows me to "Have your cake and eat it too." How many times as a child were you told: Well, you can have this or this, you can't have both. How much limitation has that created in your world?

I have many magical moment memories growing up, where the simple things were so fun and joyful. I guess I was a bit of a tomboy as I used to wrestle with my brother, who is 18 months older than me, on the front lawn. What fun we used to have. Or when we were given a stereo with records and mum would love playing old favourites from the musicals like "Oklahoma," "West Side Story" and "Sound of Music."

I have many happy memories at my grandparents' home. My grandmother was mostly in a wheelchair or on crutches as she had a bad case of osteoarthritis. She managed to cook and do what she could around the home. She spent a lot of her time sewing as this was joyful for her, and when I stayed with them I would often help with little tasks as she made all of our clothes as well as her own. What I loved was that they had a television as we didn't have one at home and after dinner at night we would watch TV and eat sweets from the lolly jar, something that we never got to do at home. Friday was shopping day and I would travel by train with my granddad to do the shopping in Fortitude Valley. This was always such an adventure for me riding on the old steam trains and I loved it when I was staying with them on a Friday.

One of our neighbours had five children and the three eldest were much older than me. One of the girls became a Home Science teacher and I would watch her ice and decorate wedding cakes and I knew the joy that that brought to me and I knew that I would one day choose to work and delight people with food. And this is exactly what I have created.

When I left school and college I worked for almost twenty years in the Creative Arts, designing and making beautiful wedding gowns, formal gowns and high end fashion working with the most opulent and decadent fabrics. This led me into the Opera, Ballet and Theatre worlds that added so much joy and fun to my life.

As a child I never felt that I fitted in anywhere. I was always wondering when my real family was going to come and find me and take me to where they lived. I guess it's like many things in this world, you just do the best that you can with the resources that you have and yet in reflection I have been willing to have so much more, and been willing to be different.

Just after I turned thirty years old, one day I woke and found myself heading into the divorce court for the second time, I had two small children and I was diagnosed with cervical cancer. That is when I started to demand some new choices.

I recognize that for the past thirty years I have been a seeker. I have done most churches, cults and religions, personal and professional development programmes on offer in this reality and yet again I always found myself once again seeking what was next. I studied a Naturopathic Diploma and owned and operated a Natural Therapies Clinic for many years. When my children were ready for university, I closed the doors of my business, sold the house and moved to Brisbane to start again. I threw myself into more modalities on offer. When I completed the process of Train the Trainer in "Neuro-Lingisitic Programming" and became a Master Hypnotherapist I thought "Wow! This is it". What a conclusion! It was the first time that I had sensed that I truly had it right. Big mistake!

When Access Consciousness® showed up some time later, because I had my answer I found it difficult to receive, yet I knew the energy was expansive and empowering. When I first met Gary Douglas, the Founder of Access Consciousness® and attended my first class with him, I just knew that this was what I was looking for, not that it was an answer. I knew that these pragmatic tools and techniques would facilitate me to have total conscious awareness.

So, here I am ten years on and I have not looked back. I love the target of Access Consciousness®, which is creating more consciousness and oneness in this world. What would it be like if more people had a target of creating a conscious world? It is the most dynamic "Change Work" I've experienced and worked with.

All of the information in this book is what I have learned in the past ten years through Access Consciousness®. One of the most powerful things that I have learned is living "as and in" the question, or being question. Were you taught that having the answer is valuable? We are literally taught in school that we had to have the RIGHT answer and we were graded on it. Questions create possibility and choices, conclusions create limitations. What if conclusions are a way of keeping us stuck in limitations?

What else is possible? How does it get any better than this?

These are two empowering questions that are used to expand the space of possibility.

Are you looking for more of you, more fun and joy, more freedom and possibility?

What if the purpose of life is to have fun?

Are you ready to Be YOU?

What if You Being You is what changes the world?

My life and living has been an interesting journey so far, and I can honestly say that I am so grateful for it all, as it has shaped me into the person that I am today. My past does not stop me from choosing so much more of me. Since my mum's passing, one thing that I have truly become aware of is that through it all, I have always known that I was born to wear diamonds and pearls. The lack, scarcity and poverty that is so abundant in this reality and what we functioned from growing up just doesn't work for me. Finding the pleasure, joy and abundance in all things is who I am as an infinite being. I am so willing to acknowledge that living from the pleasure, bliss and joy is what allows my life to keep expanding into more and more possibilities. Is this of interest to you? Would you like to be living your life of choice?

Consciousness & Oneness includes everything and judges nothing. It's the ability to be present in your life in every moment without judgement of you or anyone else. It's the ability to receive everything, to judge nothing, and to allow the entire Universe to be what it is. If you have no judgement of anything, then you get to look at everything for what it is, not for what you want it to be, not for what it ought to be, but just for what it is. From this space you can transform and change all things and create everything you desire in life—greater than what you currently have and more than what you can imagine.

~ Gary Douglas, founder of Access Consciousness®

CHAPTER TWO

Are You Ready for Something Different?

Hedonism, Decadence, Opulence, Orgasmic Living, Elegance, Aesthetics, Pleasure and Play!

What are these elements? Why are they a valuable part of life and living? What do they have to do with conscious awareness? Do you have any of these in your life? Would you like to add these elements to your life? Would you like to expand them beyond your imagination?

Hedonism is the belief in pleasure; finding the pleasure in all things. It is the willingness to experience the orgasmic quality of the joy and fun of living. It is constant pleasure-seeking—every moment of every day. It is the willingness to make your life a pleasure instead of a pain.

Opulence is about power, wealth, riches and affluence.

Decadence is immoral behaviour; the willingness to receive everything and hold onto nothing. It is the ability to waste. If you are willing to waste anything or anyone, no one will own you.

Aesthetics is the willingness to see the beauty of the moment and the change you can create or generate. Sometimes you can create a change. Sometimes you have to create a change, and sometimes you can see it as the beauty that it is without changing anything. The aesthetics is the perception of beauty.

Elegance is the willingness to use the least amount of energy to generate the maximum affect in life. . Elegance is the purity, grace, ease and gracefulness of everything. It's about the fluent and flowing.

Orgasmic Living or Liveliness is where you choose to create and generate every moment of your life from the fun, joy and intensely expansive energies. It is not to live your life, but to have a life that is lively—one that is continuously expanding and generating. It means that you add a lot to your life, and you have the joy and the fun of living, not just the work and the drudgery. Most people think that if you are not working really hard, you are not doing your job. Too many jobs to get done does not mean you are having a life. It means you are doing a lot of work.

Liveliness is also the **ability to have.** It is the ability to see what choices there are in the world. You all have had the experience of living from liveliness.

How often do you allow yourself to choose something for the pure pleasure of it...without judgement? How often do you choose to live your life from the adventure of what could show up, rather than the conclusion of what you or someone else decided should be?

Ask yourself, "If I were truly living today from the total joy and adventure of being alive what would I choose?"

If you could have the exuberant, unbounded joy you had before you learned to judge it as wrong, what else would be possible?

Are you willing to explore this very unreal, unbelievable, fantastic and phenomenal possibility for a way of living that has never been seen or experienced on the planet before?

Hedonism, the pursuit of pleasure, is one of the most judgeable offenses on planet earth.

In the past, people have deemed hedonism, opulence and decadence as bad things, instead of recognising that if you use these elements correctly; you will actually have more blessings show up in your life. By definition, hedonism is the belief that pleasure or happiness is the highest good—a devotion to pleasure as a way of life—which is not a bad thing, it is actually just the willingness to make your life a pleasure instead of a struggle. And decadence, well that is defined as unrestrained or excessive self-indulgence, immoral behaviour, but really it is the willingness to receive everything without judgement. Opulence is all about power, wealth, riches and affluence. For what reason are these elements seen as bad?

What if these elements are about creating and generating your life and living as *choice*?

Isn't it interesting that when we actually read these words: hedonism, decadence, opulence and orgasmic living, the first thing which pops into our minds is to do with money? And we go, "OMG, I don't have the money to do or have all of that."

I live in a beautiful apartment that overlooks Brisbane River, and I am so grateful for it every day. Living there allows me to find pleasure in walking along the river's edge and having a cool breeze and the sun on my skin. I find pleasure in having ducks waddle up to me with that energetic connection. I find the pleasure and joy in just sitting and watching the Brisbane City Cats (Catamarans) glide up and down the river with their passengers on board, on their way to work or some other event. Or I enjoy taking a walk at night and having the city lights shimmering on the river.

Finding these pleasures doesn't necessarily cost money. It is truly just a choice to find the pleasure in all things. Pleasure is all about the gratification of the senses; it's excitement, it is happiness produced by enjoyment. We receive pleasure from the indulgence of our appetite; from the view of a beautiful landscape; from the harmony of sounds; from the expectation of seeing an absent friend; from the prospect

of gain or success of any kind. Pleasure, bodily and mentally, consti-
tutes the whole of happiness. The Play element is about putting into
motion and action. It's about actioning and actualizing our choices.
These are all of the elements that are the source of having a generative and phenomenal life.

Having a Generative Life

If you are truly choosing to have a generative life you must use
the elements of elegance, aesthetics, decadence, hedonism, opulence,
pleasure, play and liveliness.

Generating and creating your life is a choice. You have a choice
of the creation of life—which is you being energy, space, consciousness, and then adding matter and time—and you can generate a
life—which is you being energy, space and consciousness. (We will
expand on this a little later). If you generate your life, you will also
create your life. You don't do just one or the other. So when you are
being energy, space and consciousness, that is where the sparks of
possibility live. These are the ideas, mostly of which no one has even
considered before. An example of that would be—you would like to
write a book, so the spark of possibility would be the topic of which
you would like to write about, the idea for the book. Then to create
the book, you have to add matter and time. The matter is the words
on the pages and the time is the time that it takes to put the words
on the pages. Then there is the institution, which is what is required
to keep the book being created.

If I stopped writing now would this book ever get finished? The
institution of me continuing to write is what is then creating the
book until it is ready for the next stage.

Are you willing to create? Are you willing to generate? Are you
willing to do it all, from these elements of generation? These are the
ways in which you can create your life instead of creating a reality. A
reality is created when two people either align and agree, which is

acceptance, or resist and react to a point of view, and it is interesting when this shows up.

I am currently creating a book (apart from this one), about food, sex and bodies, and having a lot of fun with it as I truly enjoy cooking and nurturing bodies with great-tasting food. As I have been cooking the food I have been photographing it and every now and again posting some of the photos on social media. I have been choosing this mostly for the fun and also to create an interest in the future possibility of making sales of the book.

Today I received an email from a long-time friend reacting to the photographs, saying that they lack colour and appeal. What she was really saying was that they were not good enough for a cookbook. The subject line in the email stated "Your cookbook, very impressive." Is that a mixed message? Is that creating a reality that may limit me if I choose to let it? If I choose to align and agree or resist or react to her points of view then I have created a reality of limitation that then I could use to diminish me and put me into doubt and then choose to stop creating the book.

When you are creating your own reality you are crystal clear in what you are choosing, and anyone impelling and pushing you with their point of view will not affect you or put you into doubt of your choices.

When you are doing the elegance, aesthetics, decadence, hedonism and liveliness of things, then you have no judgement. Then you can have everything. If you can have everything, would you then ever have any more problems? If you had so much money that nothing mattered to you, you would be considered decadent and yet it's the willingness to receive *everything,* so much so that nothing is more important than anything else. From that the one thing I know for sure is that when I am not creating my life of choice, it is very easy to judge. Is that working for you?

Are You Living in a Contracted Reality?

If you want to know what it feels like to contract your life, think about how someone who judges you would like you to live your life. Do you get the sense of being squashed and mutilated? That is a contracted reality, whereby you end up trying to be the same as everyone else, while destroying you and your body in the process.

A friend of mine has a daughter who has always said as long as I have known her that getting married and having children wasn't of interest to her. However, now that she is in her thirties, her parents, siblings and friends keep on telling her all the time that she has a great boyfriend, and as you have been together for 10 years it is time to get married and have children. When you are at the age when all of your siblings and friends are getting married and having children, how much expectation is there for you to choose the same thing? So now you are experiencing pressure to be the same as everyone else.

But, what if you can have a different life and reality? Would you be willing to choose what works for you and not bend under the pressure of the people who say they love you? Do they really love you or are they judging you and your choices? When you are contracting your reality to fit in with other people's points of view, you are destroying you and your body. What if you can have liveliness and joy and the freedom to choose what works for you?

"Indulge, but Refine"

There is a set of books called *The Alexandria Quartet* by Lawrence Durrell, which are great reading and I highly recommend. It's a set of novels about Alexandria in the 1920's and 1930's, written from four different points of view about the same events. You begin to see how "interesting point of view" is such a necessity, because each one of them takes only their own point of view to describe what they see and perceive. I have not walked a thousand miles in any other person's shoes (nor would I choose to as that would lead to mimicking), so how can I judge them and their choices as I do not see life through their eyes. There is a quote in the book that says, "The purpose of life is to indulge, but refine." If you do indulgence, refining your indulgence, you will never go to decadence as destructive or hedonism as pain.

Now can you see how a decadent hedonistic life is one that is full of liveliness and is the source of having a generative and phenomenal life? Who wouldn't want that? Perhaps you have already been trying to *create* a phenomenal life for yourself but it just isn't showing up. Did you realise that creation has a polar opposite, which is destruction? However, there is no polar opposite to generation as it is continually creative—when you generate something, you give it life, and once you give something life, it continues to create more of its own life. Generating a life might work easier for you—hedonistic, opulent, decadent, orgasmic living!

I know I am asking you to change a lot of your thinking, however once you do, you will start to generate that opulent, decadent and orgasmic living you have desired for so long. Are you willing to break down more of the constructs you have been living from and really get to the fun generative stuff? Imagine if you could create more from the pleasure and joy than without it!

Does waking up on a morning to an amazing sunrise open up your being and heart? If not, then perhaps something needs to change.

Questions to Empower You...

- Am I willing to make my life a pleasure?
- What points of view do I have that are creating the limitations of my reality?
- Am I being in allowance, as everything is just an interesting point of view?

- Begin to choose by asking, "Will this be rewarding?"
- What is it that truly brings me pleasure?
- What is it that truly brings me joy?
- What is it that truly turns me and my body on?
- What is it that when I am doing it I have a sense of being fully alive?
- Would you like to have the true pleasure of being fully alive?
- Would you like to increase the level of pleasure in your life? What about your work life and your love life? And more importantly would you like to increase the level of joy moment by moment, day by day?
- Would you like to have access to the pleasure of being alive?
- Do the birds wake up and not sing because they are having a bad hair day?
- Have you been told that joy is something that you can't have?

What if?

- What if joy could be an actual living and breathing actualization of you in this world with every possibility that you have ever hoped for brought into existence?
- What if this world and your body are meant to be enjoyed?

A Hedonist is one who goes so far as to enjoy everything totally, but never goes so far that they are incapable of enjoying what could come next.

~ Gary Douglas

CHAPTER THREE

Creating Your Life of Choice

What is that exactly, I hear you ask? Do you even have the concept of what creating your life of choice actually is? Or do you feel like a ship without a rudder, being tossed and thrown about in your life's journey, being at the effect of others and their choices.

First, you need to realise that your *point of view creates your reality*. Your reality does not create your point of view! We are taught to either align or agree with things, or resist and react to them: I like this person, I don't like this person; opulence is good, opulence is bad; this house is good, this house is bad. I have to make the right choice, or I will be judged for making the wrong choice. All of this is judgement and polarity; however there is another option —*"allowance."* If you can be in allowance, then you are the rock in the stream and nothing and no one can affect you, whereas if you are functioning from judgement you are creating limitations. The best tool to use when you feel judgement coming up is to see the situation as "an interesting point of view." If everything were just an interesting point of view, there would be no need for you to align and agree or resist and react to anything, and once that happens, you will suddenly start moving into a place of no context; you will be total choice, question, possibility and contribution.

Once you have moved to a place of allowance, you can begin to choose. At first, it may not be easy to fathom that everything is a choice. People believe they have no choice. For example, you might say, "I have no choice; I have to go to work." No, you actually have a choice - you can call in sick, choose not to pay your rent for the week, choose not to buy food, choose not to purchase things that add to your life. Just because you chose not to be hungry and go to work, doesn't mean you did not make a choice. It is just a matter of how you look at it because everything is a choice. Even no choice is a choice. How much do you believe you are in a "no choice" position because the choice you made was not really your choice?

Most people try to logically figure out what the best choice is going to be to ensure nothing will go wrong when they make the "right" choice. Let's just look at this for a moment! When you spend that much effort and consideration, you end up with a point of view (remember, that's what creates your reality) and the underlying point of view is that something bad is going to happen, so you choose the opposite. That is an interesting point of view!

With the point of view that something bad is going to happen as a result of your choice, that is creation and destruction in action— you are trying to create the thing that will not destruct.

As I sit here writing this I have the awareness of the choice that I made to come to Bali, Indonesia and promote my work as part of the Bali Spirit Festival. It cost a few thousand dollars for a return trip here, accommodation, food and the festival fees and expenses. After two days and very little showing up, it would be easy to go into how I made a wrong choice. However, I know that there are no wrong choices, just choice creates awareness. So I am in the question of what else is possible here. What else can I create and generate? It is interesting that this is creating the space for me to write this book that I have been talking about for a long time. I am also willing to make a new choice, which is perhaps me choosing to leave for home earlier than my set flight date. Everything is a choice and there is no right or wrong choice.

Ironically, you make a choice, something changes but you decide you must live by your choice because really we've all been taught that there are always consequences to our actions (choices). What if that was a lie and the only consequence of choice is awareness? If you change from choosing between right and wrong, to choosing between yes and no, then you can never make a wrong choice. You simply need to ask yourself, "Will I choose this?" and wait until you sense a yes or no, or "If I choose this what will my life be like in five years?" and "If I don't choose this what will my life be like in five years?" Then you can make rewarding choices for you. What if you never made choices from the "no money, no time or I am sick" points of view? These are the three things that everyone uses to not choose what they truly desire.

Don't get caught up in believing that you will now only make the "best choice" for you. Best choice is a judgement, and it doesn't mean you will always benefit, as rewarding and benefitting are not the same things. It just means you will begin to choose for you, instead of making choices based on other people's thoughts, feelings and emotions. Choosing what's rewarding can include everyone, just not their points of view. Interestingly, you can't have awareness before you choose and you can't get awareness unless you choose.

About 15 years ago when I had my Natural Therapies business in Central Queensland, I was burnt out and desperate for something different in my life. Every day I would ask the universe to give me the awareness of what was next for me. Thank goodness I didn't get what I was asking for, as I was in so much judgement of myself that I wasn't getting it, that I asked for a barbeque to drop on my head so that it would be that obvious. I know I am cute not bright. I was so paralyzed in the "NO CHOICE" universe for fear that I was going to make another wrong choice, as that is all that I had been fed my entire life--"You have made another wrong choice." I wasn't willing to just choose and have the awareness of that choice. Eventually I did and I am so grateful for it wasn't long after that I moved to Brisbane, and Access Consciousness® showed up in my life.

Choice Creates Awareness; Awareness Does Not Create Choice

What if every choice that you make creates a cobweb of future potentials? Do you know that every time you ask a question, you create possibilities? When the possibility and the potential intersect, you create a new reality. When choice intersects question, a new reality gets created. It can be as simple as making a choice to take a different route to go to your job and missing an accident. The question intercepts choice, so a different reality gets created. Please get that you always have choice.

Choice Is Ultimately the Source of Awareness

You don't have to include everybody in your choice. You just choose, and when you choose from consciousness that choice will include everyone.

Are you looking for "What do I choose?" Are you looking through everybody else's reality to find out what you are going to choose? Were you always taught to do it this way? Did it really work? Are you trying to find your reality through your parents' reality, and yet you are nothing like them? Do you ever ask, "Am I like any of them? Do I want to choose to be like them?" You go, "Where can I find in them what I need to know about me?" What you need to know about you has nothing to do with any of them. Are you spending your entire life trying to look through their realities, thinking you are going to find yours?

Just before you step into realizing what you would really like to have, it feels like there is a void, because everything you have decided is real or true based on this reality disappears. Then you have the next moment to live the rest of your life—choose. Choice creates potentials. Question creates possibilities. When possibility intersects a potential, a new reality gets created. So you have to be willing to choose and question until you find the new reality that is you.

Do you know that you are the source of you, or are you always looking for how somebody else can give you an awareness of you? You cannot see you as long as you have no idea what is true and valuable for you. You can't choose for you unless you have an awareness of what your point of view is. You can only choose against someone else or for someone else because you are not in the computation of your life.

You tend to keep defining and judging what would make your life that you're OK with, better. What if it was ok to be ok with the life you have and have no point of view about it? Then you'd be satisfied. That's not possible in this reality. You're never supposed to be satisfied. Do you always want more? Desiring more doesn't necessarily mean desiring more of this reality. Do you desire more awareness, more capacity, and more of all kinds of things?

Choice made from being is different than choice from doing. If you are willing to be vilified, every choice is available to you. If you are not willing to be judged, you must do judgement in order to choose. You have to choose that which is not judgeable which means you have to judge that every choice you make is going to be judged.

When you just choose, it's from being. When you choose something "because..." it's from doing.

Awareness is not clarity. If you have clarity then you have made a decision. From awareness you can choose anything. When you have clarity you know you are going to choose the right thing. That's conclusion.

People say, "I'm choosing this." Or "I've chosen this." That is not choosing; that's coming to conclusion that you have chosen. Choice is only good for that one moment. There's no choice in "I've chosen."

Concluding what to choose before you choose is not choice, it is judgement. What feels light? Ok, do that. That's true choice.

Are you doubting your choices, your awareness? Do you double-check instead of just being aware? Are you willing to give up your doubt?

If you trust your awareness, when there is something wonky with the choice, you will sense it and you will ask for more information of what is going on so you can change something. For example, you are planning a weekend away with friends, and two weeks leading into the weekend no-one has committed and you have paid a non-refundable deposit, so you choose to cancel the trip. What if this then opens the path to something else greater showing up? Perhaps something that you have been asking for some time! So instead of doubting your choice, always be willing to make a new choice in the next moment.

It can feel really uncomfortable to just follow the energy, so we tend to want to solidify it to make it comfortable. Give it up. Go on the adventure!

When you have a difficulty with a choice, indulge the idea of everything you think is wrong about it. To indulge it, you go into your head and do everything in your life as if that was your choice. It's being in the question of, "What would this be like?" After two or three days, you begin to see the reality of what that would be like rather than the fantasy reality you were hoping it would be. Indulge your choice energetically and you will get the awareness of what you really want to choose.

Many of us act as though no choice is more real to us than choice. It's just a choice. "You know what? Damn it! I'm going to go into this intensity and see what comes out the other side." Every point of view you have about what you can't do is like a rabbit hole. If you go through it you will get to another universe. So jump in and go YEE-HAH!

Don't make having choice the most valuable choice. Choice is just choice. You can choose again and again and again.

Questions to Empower You

- What if the only consequence of choice is awareness?

- Is this a rewarding choice?

- What if every choice I make was not right or wrong but exactly what is required for me to become as aware as I truly am now?

- What if there is no right or wrong choice, just choice creates awareness?

- If I never made a wrong choice, what choice would I have? Infinite choice.

- What part of this reality am I unwilling to lose, that if I would lose it would step me into a different reality in which I could totally choose?

What if?

- What if you indulged in choice?

- What if you were aware of your true value?

- What if you created your life instead of just existing in it?

- What if you knew that you were not the effect of anything?

We are always trying to make the good choice, the best choice, thinking that if we make the best choice then everything is going to come out a certain way. We are so vested in creating a result that we forget to create. If you have no result in mind, what you can create is greater than what you know. if you have a result in mind, you can't get anything better than that.

~ Gary Douglas

CHAPTER FOUR

Creating from the Hedonist's Guide to Opulent, Decadent and Orgasmic Living

- Are you willing to receive everything as a contribution to your life?

- All energies (good, bad and ugly) are a contribution to your life if you are willing to receive it all as an interesting point of view, all of which is allowance and no judgement.

- Do you wear beautiful jewels with precious stones and fine fabrics of silk and linen that contribute to you and your body?

- Do you have luxurious furnishings, like a delicious bed that your body just loves getting into? Do you eat tasty treats of delicious food that allows your taste buds to orgasm?

- Are you willing to have it all?

This goes way beyond having possessions, and is actually about what you are willing to *"receive"*—the sensation of amazing fabrics against your body or the admiring glances from people passing by—this all adds to your enjoyment of life in every area.

You can have a life where these things are a priority for you and everything is a pleasure.

Would you be willing not to be worried about what others think about you and your choices for living? To have this will require that you give up every answer you have decided and concluded as having either as right or wrong. You will have to embrace living, instead of maintaining the illusion of having a life. So to be able to embrace this, let's look at what receiving is.

What Is Receiving All About?

Receiving isn't *"having,"* it is actually awareness; it is getting the energy of everything and being aware of it all without any points of view. True receiving is being able to receive all the information that there is. Receiving doesn't have to do with money. It has to do with everything. It has to do with the awareness of everything that is possible. When you truly are able to receive, you are able to be in the question. Do you know that the universe can only give you what you can receive? Can you only receive how messed up you are? This is especially true when things don't show up the way that you have decided they should. So if you were asking for more money to show up in your life, do you acknowledge that more money is showing up when someone buys you a meal, or a glass of wine, or even when you are given clothes that someone no longer desires to have? Are you aware that all of this is money? If you have already decided that money is cash in your hands or in your bank account then you can't acknowledge that the universe has your back and is gifting to you what you asked for, just in a different form. How often have you thought that things in your life haven't worked out for you? But is that really true or has it worked out exactly the way you have created it? You have to be brutally honest with yourself and know that you did it all—everything in your life is your creation, good, bad and ugly. Once you acknowledge that then you can create something greater. So when you request something of the universe, that then is the beginning of generation.

Several years ago I woke one morning with the awareness of asking, "I wonder what it would be like to have too much money in my life." I got on with my day facilitating a class without any considerations of what I had asked for earlier. On my lunchbreak I dashed out to do some chores, you know those usual last-minute-just-before-you-travel things to do like banking and picking up the dry cleaning, as I was leaving for overseas the next day. As I was crossing the road I got this energetic pull to look down at the road. As I did I noticed a small object sitting there. I bent down to see what it was and as I reached to pick it up I realised I was picking up a ring with the most beautiful brilliant diamond that has since been valued at $10,000.

"Ask and you shall receive" is a truth. We generate and create by requesting of the universe; by asking, you are not manifesting. Manifestation is the how it shows up, so you don't manifest, you create and generate all by asking questions. You be and receive in simultaneity so you have to *be* the energy in order to *receive* it. When you are willing to be anything, you can *have* anything. When you are trying to *have* things, and you are not willing to *be* them, then you can't get them. You have to be the vibration of gold in order to have gold. You have to be the vibration of money to have money. If you are willing to be those things, money just starts to come from all kinds of directions.

Have you ever noticed that when you become the vibration of sex, everybody wants to touch your body? If you want something in your life, *be* the vibration that will allow it to come to you, because if you are not being it, you cannot invite it and it cannot show up in your life. People who have money don't hang out with poor people. If you hang out with rich people, you get richer, because rich people believe in having money, being money and creating more and gen-erating more. People who are poor believe in having nothing, doing nothing, creating nothing and instituting as little as possible. Where do you want to live? What are you inviting to your life, possibilities or something much less?

My son has recently been home visiting. He works as a corporate Lawyer and is a partner in a worldwide corporate law firm. He has such an ease with and around money. He gets to wheel and deal with billions of dollars every day and is the energy and vibration of money. Every conversation we had he showed me constantly the "what else is possible?" with money. He doesn't worry about money nor does he make money significant. He enjoys it and plays with it and uses it to change people's lives. When we went to restaurants, when it was time to order, he never looked at the right side of the menu. Price never comes into his choices. If he wants something, then he gets it. He once said to me, "Mum, I never let what other people think about me, get to me. It is just their point of view." He is such a gift to my life.

In my own life, whenever I am willing to step into something greater and be more of me, then so much more of everything begins to show up. More money, more joy, more fun and everything that I ask for. Stepping into something greater may be scary for some people! Are you willing to receive the contribution of all energies to bring you more in your life? Would you be willing to receive as a contribution the energies of judgement to bring more into your life?

Last year I did a seven-week telecall series on "Having Your Cake and Eating It Too." I had over 700 registrations for the first call which I offered for free. Within minutes of finishing the first call I had emails of gratitude arriving in my inbox. A day later I received an email from someone who wrote a page of judgements about me and the class that I facilitated. As I was willing to receive all of her judgements as an interesting point of view, the intensity of all that energy allowed so much more to show up in my life and my life got greater as a result. If I had gone into the wrongness of the person for sending me such a terrible email, or the wrongness of me for what

I said on the call from her point of view, then I would have put up the defences to receiving and my life would have been diminished.

So now let's talk about how caring and receiving plays a role in all of this.

Do you spend a lot of your life trying to care for everyone? Do these people really desire the caring that you have for them? True caring is giving people only what they can receive. You can only care for people to the degree that they are willing to receive it. People, who cannot receive, cannot receive. They desire something different from you. Do you feel drained and depleted when you are trying to give what someone cannot receive?

I have spent a very large part of my life caring for others. This first started when I was a child and being around my mother as she was suffering from her disease. I refused to be aware of what she and others could receive and I constantly felt like I had the bone marrow sucked out of my bones. When I was operating my Natural Health Clinic, at the end of each day my body felt like a hundred Mack trucks had run over it. Now I am aware of how much caring I was trying to give people that they couldn't and refused to receive. Who do you have in your life that is refusing to receive the caring that you have for them?

Recently I had a person in my life who I truly cared about. I opened my home to her and was kind and caring to her. What I failed to be aware of was that she had no concept of what true kindness and caring was, or what it was to have someone who functioned from that. She only knew her value through abuse. That first started from her mother and then from all of the relationships that she has had with the men in her life. She is constantly trying to prove how caring and kind she is, and generally when someone is trying to prove something it is because they have decided that they are the opposite of that.

When someone thinks they are really mean they can find out that they are really kind and caring people. They have just been in such judgement of themselves their whole lives and then their life changes and this is one of the greatest gifts that there is.

What I have noticed is that when people say that they are really kind, they are usually really mean. When someone is trying to prove they are the sweetest person on the planet, they are hiding the fact that they are not.

People always try to prove the opposite of what they really are.

As a result of not being able to receive the caring that I had for her she has now created separation and exclusion from me. What she is unwilling to get is that I am so grateful for her and her choices, as it has empowered me to have so much more awareness of where people function from. It has allowed me to have so much more caring and kindness for me.

So now let's look at what caring you have for you. Do you have a concept of what that really is? If you really cared for you would you be worried about what other people think about you and your choices? If you were really willing to be taken care of, then would you allow the universe to contribute to you? Your level of caring describes your ability to receive. When you have a dynamic level of caring you can receive a whole lot more. What would it be like if you would be that level of caring for you? Would the walls vanish so you could be and receive everything with total choice? What would that be like? Are you willing to have that much caring for you?

When you care about things (your car, house, job) greater than you care about you, is it because you have decided they are an extension of you? So are they really you, or are they your creations? Have you decided that the creation *is* you and is greater than you so you won't destroy it or lose it to create or generate something different? Have you decided that having those things equals caring? In making those things more valuable than you, you will only change them a little to keep them in existence. Would you be willing to lose everything to have all of you? What you are unwilling to lose gets to control you!

I was a single mum from when my two children were small, and I had made my children so important and significant that they got to control me totally and I was unwilling to lose them, which meant that I could never get to be me, as I was always trying to be the person that they wanted me to be. Did this keep me in constant judgement of me? Absolutely. At this point please get that you don't have to create to lose them, you just have to be willing to lose them, which is very different. So it wasn't until I realised how much their judgements of me and my choices were destroying me that I knew that I had to start making some new choices that included me in the computation. Who would I be without my kids and the single mum status? How many identities and personas had I created with this? Who would I be without the "I raised them all by myself" martyrdom? It took me years to see, that while I was unwilling to lose them I got to destroy me in the process, as I wasn't willing to receive their judgements as an interesting point of view. When I was willing to lose them, and that did show up; when we all looked at what we were creating, we were then willing to change it and create something different. Their allowance of me and my choices is now very different. How does it get any better than this?

What Are You Refusing?

What if everything that was possible in the world was available at your request? It is, so how much are you refusing it? In order to not receive, you have to refuse to ask. Are you refusing to ask, are you refusing to receive, and are you refusing to be everything that would allow the things in your life to come to fruition?

Do you tend to refuse the gift of what you have decided you will not be? Are you refusing to be the gift of you on planet earth?

Are you refusing to be the catalyst for change? What energies are you refusing to be and receive?

For example, if you will not be money, you will refuse the gift that money is. When you say, "I don't want to do that," are you refusing to be the source of power and potency that can provide everything for everyone? Do you have people who want you to be the source for their money or their life? What if you become the question, the catalyst, the potency and the power that allows them to look at themselves differently: What question can you be, that would allow you to generate that in your life?

A Question Empowers; an Answer Dis-empowers

Ask questions that empower the person to see what they can be, what they know, what they perceive, what they can receive and what they're refusing to be, to know, to perceive and receive. If you do that, then you are the source that contributes to everything and everyone.

Have you always thought that you had to be the source, contribution and the power that gave people what they needed, wanted and desired? Do you always know what other people's needs, requirements and desires are? Do you know what your needs, requirements and desires are?

Anybody that comes to you with any need, want or desire, really requires of you the only thing that you can actually gift to them: that is awareness.

Questions to Empower You

- Am I being present and aware of all energies?
- Am I receiving all energies as an interesting point of view?
- Am I refusing to receive?
- Am I giving people that which they can't receive?
- Do I have kindness and caring for me?

What if?

- What if you were willing to be true caring for you?

- What if you were willing to be the catalyst, potency and change that allow you and others to be all of themselves?

- What if you were willing to ask for everything that you truly desired to show up in your life?

- What if you were so open and vulnerable that your vibration was an invitation for others to create happiness?

Receiving is not a flow towards you. It is a stepping into everything that is available to you.

~ Gary Douglas

CHAPTER FIVE

The Elements of Contribution

Contribution is a two-way street—as you gift, so shall you receive.

Help is a one-way street in which, at the end of it, you get to demand something in return.

Helping is doing. With help, you are trying to create an obligation with the other person. Help just means you get to prove that you are superior. I know better than you do, so just do it my way. With contribution by doing what you are doing or contributing what you are contributing, you are actually expanding your own life, even though you don't understand how that is so.

Help is very much what I was raised to do. Everything was about "You are here to help others!" Being raised in strict Catholicism, I was always told to put others first and see the good in everyone. Consciousness includes everything without judgement, good bad and ugly. When you are only looking for the good, you can never see the bad and ugly when it shows up and then you get to be at the effect of the bad and ugly. These points of view that I took on allowed me to destroy, lose and divorce me totally. And it has been an amazing journey discovering me again. Do you desire to discover you again?

Contribution is not cognitive, however help is. People who help only want to deliver a little bit, with the idea that they are going to get something back. People who are contributing never care whether they get anything back. They just really enjoy the process of contributing. Some people think they are helping when they are contributing. And some people think that they are contributing when they aren't doing anything at all.

If you refuse to contribute and receive contribution, you stop all contribution and try to do everything all by yourself. If you do it all by yourself, you eliminate any kind of relationship except somebody who wants to take from you.

This is where I was at, and my life became a self-fulfilling prophecy, "I have to do it all by myself." The majority of people who showed up in my life were the takers. It wouldn't matter how much I had to give they always wanted more, and it was still not enough from their point of view. I have spent a large majority of my life doing it all by myself, with the lack of receiving the contribution of others. I was always so busy giving; I now realise that I had a total refusal to receive. I was living my life from a ledger system. If someone bought me a coffee or a meal I always remembered that it was my turn to pay the next time. Or I would always be the first person to open my wallet so that I could refuse the gifting so as not to create an obligation with the other person. Cute not bright, what can I say!

Help requires somebody to see you as less than them. Contribution is the willingness to receive from everyone who is willing to contribute to you, and being willing to contribute to those who are willing to receive. It's a two-way street. But if you do it all by yourself, then you must cut off any awareness that would contribute to you.

Contribution is not a doing, but you can do to contribute. Contribution is when it's a joy to do things. When you hate doing them, it's because you're not being a contribution, you're delivering something you don't really want to do—and that's help.

When I had my clinic, people who worked for me would say that they were contributing, and I couldn't understand why I would get angry. It was because it was lie, which is why I would get angry with them. A lie will always make you angry. Often, they were not a contribution. They wanted to help only to the degree that they got enough money to make their life work the way they wanted it to. I have had many people work for me and the sole purpose was to get money so that they could have the life that they thought was abundant. I now choose people who are contributory and they work *with* me not *for* me.

What I now know, is that the real contribution that they were making to me was the judgement that I had too much money. Now that's the judgement that's going to make me more money. That's a great contribution. I no longer had to be angry, because it was no longer about taking my money; they were actually contributing to making me more money.

Contribution and Creation

The basic elements of creation are question, choice, possibility and contribution. Have we made contribution the most important element of this? Question, choice and possibility are also required to generate anything and everything in your life. What we do is we give up question, choice and possibility in favour of contribution because we feel it is more important to contribute, and to be contributed to, than anything else. We place greater value on the contribution that we believe someone is, something is, or some choice is, that will provide for us more than we value awareness.

You wouldn't choose anything unless you had the point of view that it was a contribution to your life, living and reality. The trouble is that what you think is the contribution is often 180 degrees from what the actual contribution of being that way actually is. There is not just positive contribution there is also negative contribution. We have been programmed to believe that contribution is everything and that contribution is what you have to give to others or what you have to receive from others. Contribution is actually "as you gift, so shall you receive," but that point of view does not exist in this reality. So what have you focussed on as what contribution is: "Why aren't I getting everything I want? Why isn't there more for me?"

Contribution is seen as giving and taking; as what you can or can't get and what must or can't give, when it is really the combination of gifting and receiving simultaneously. Contribution is being and receiving and it is gifting and receiving at the same time.

When you make contribution more valuable (your contribution to others or their contribution to you) you are excluding the possibility of you choosing something different. There is no question, choice or possibility in there so it is no longer about awareness.

Rather than go to question, choice and possibility to give you more awareness, we make contribution the conclusion. "I have to contribute" or "I can't contribute" which become your only choices. This excludes all the other elements of creation. You spend all your energy looking at what someone contributes or doesn't contribute and what you have to contribute or what you don't want to contribute, and there is no question in any of that.

Contribution and Awareness—What a Gift!

Contribution is not having a judgement about what you cannot be or cannot know. If you take the point of view, "I don't know anything about food or cooking, so I can't really contribute to this," then you are cutting off every possibility of knowing about food and its gift to the body and you cannot receive from anything that is connected to food.

If you are not willing to receive the contribution of the food, then you have to have a problem with your body. Everything is interrelated. There is nothing you couldn't know about. Why not know everything?

When I studied Naturopathy, I was impelled with millions of points of view about the right and wrong foods, the good and bad foods. Sugar is bad, gluten and wheat are bad. Always eat raw green food, as that is good for you. There was always the right or wrong diet. These judgements of food took me away from being totally aware of what my body and other bodies required as healing, caring and nurturing elements. Decisions, judgements and conclusions take you out of awareness into total limitations.

What does contribution mean to you? Do you think that you have to do something and put your time into something in order to contribute? You don't have to be with anything to be a contribution to it. If you're a contribution to it, then you also have to be willing to receive from it.

Are you willing to contribute to anything and receive all the awareness that it has to give you about any aspect of what it is, who it is, where it is, when it is, how it is or that it is? Are you willing to have the awareness of everything? Are you cutting off awareness? Most people try to cut off awareness in order to feel that they are not doing too much, or to make sure that they do the right thing that's going to create the result they are looking for. Do you only make decisions to get a result? What if you contributed to everything as a way of creating a different possibility, a different reality?

What if everything we are willing to contribute to and *be a part of* creates a different reality? That is oneness and consciousness.

If you take the point of view, "I don't like someone," then you aren't willing to contribute to them. Then the end result is that you diminish your capacity to know anything that they are aware of at all. Contribution doesn't mean you have to contribute to making them successful. That's different. Most people think that either you are a contribution and everything you do is wonderful and positive, or that you are not a contribution and then you want to destroy the person. In oneness, nothing dies. Even the body doesn't die—it just transforms into something else. Does it become food for the worms? Can you stop contributing to anything really? Are you sticking yourself with that lie? By not ever refusing to be aware of anything, you are a contribution to everything.

Contribution to mean people can be, "What can I do to expose to everyone how mean they are?" You want to contribute to mean people everything that allows them to be as mean as they truly are. Otherwise, you shut so much of you off, trying not to contribute to mean people.

Rather than trying to fix people's problems and give them solutions, how can you be a contribution that allows them to be everything that would give them what they desire? If you try to fix people's financial problems or problems with their body, they will not become aware of what they need to become aware of. Are you always trying to do things for people as though that is contribution?

Fixing people's bodies and their problems I know all about. One of my most favourite songs by Cold Play is called "Fix You."

Several years ago before I came across Access Consciousness®, I met a man who was going through a very messy marriage break up. He was referred to me as a client. After our working agreement finished we remained friends and some years later we worked together on some wealth empowerment seminars. He asked if we could get together to create a relationship. I kept on saying no for quite some time and then after a while I eventually agreed. My body was constantly facilitating his body. He was about 10 years younger than me and yet looked 10 plus years older. Whenever I spent time with him, my body would feel like a hundred Mach trucks had run over it and it would feel much heavier like I had added 10 kilos. He would always say, "Wow, whenever I have time with you I feel so much younger and it's like I lose about 10 kilos." I was fixing his life and body at a huge cost to me. I wasn't empowering him to have his own awareness of his life and body. After several months of this I became aware of what I was choosing and made a new choice. I saw him approximately two years later and he had re-married. He was very unhappy and he had aged quite considerably. Empowering people with question is more expansive than trying to fix them.

Contribution is an integral part of who you choose to be. You have to destroy you dynamically in order to not be a contribution to everything.

Contribution requires a degree of receiving before you have the ability to gift. Only if you have the ability to receive what somebody can receive can you gift anything to them. In this reality everybody is trying to create exchange. In oneness, there is no exchange. It just is. In oneness, everything is received before it is given. In contribution there is simultaneity of gifting and receiving.

You can only cut off your awareness of what can be received; you never cut off the capacity to receive. Do you refuse to receive everything so that you can continue to be limited?

Are you looking to see how this reality can contribute to your reality? This reality may not contribute to your reality, but without the contribution, you are excluding your awareness so you can exclude this reality.

If you were willing to let this reality work for you and your reality, then instead of judging you, seeing the wrongness of you, or seeing what people are doing to you, you start to see how every single solitary person is a contribution to you. That's how you eliminate the separation and the judgement that exists between people. If you judge me: thank you for the contribution. If you hate me: thank you for the contribution. If you love me: thank you for the contribution.

If you give me money: thank you for the contribution. Then you are always willing to receive exactly what is going on.

When you contribute, whether it be energy, money or whatever you choose to contribute, it changes what was in existence. Then you get to have the awareness of what you changed by what you chose. The ultimate contribution is choice and question. Quantum contribution is where you realise that there is nothing you can't contribute, there is nothing you can't be, there is nothing you can't do, there is nothing you can't gift and nothing you can't receive.

Quantum Contribution Is You Being You

Have you ever noticed that you are always trying to figure out what you don't have or what you need or what's wrong with you? When you are willing to be all of you in every moment you are being "quantum contribution." **QUAN"TUM,** n. [L.] The quantity; the amount.

What if you were willing to be a quantum contribution to everything? Would there be anything that you couldn't be? Would there be anything that you couldn't do? Would there be anything that you couldn't have? Would there be anything that you couldn't create? Would there be anything that you couldn't generate? Would there be anything that you couldn't institute? How potent would you be then?

If you truly desire to have the magnificent life you could have, you need to be willing to be the contribution to everything. To be the contribution to everything means you are going to have to be willing to receive anything and everything without a point of view.

Refusing Contribution

As soon as I was willing and started to be a contribution to me, I realised that I was being a contribution to everyone and to the earth.

Are you willing to be a contribution to you? The one thing most of us try to do is give to others, but are you willing to include you in that? You are the greatest contribution you can be to yourself.

Have you ever noticed the energy that an animal gives you? Do you receive that energy easily? How many people give that kind of energy to you? Most people aren't capable of contributing to anyone, including themselves. Plants and animals contribute to us magnificently. Living in the countryside or by the ocean is nurturing and caring of your body and soul. But anywhere you are can be a contribution to you. We tend to decide, "I don't like that, so I don't want that contribution." How much of what is nurturing and caring to you and your body are you refusing?

What points of view have you made so solid and real, that if you would change them, would manifest as total contribution to you, to the world and to being all of you?

I love visiting my daughter's home on the Gold Coast. There is something about the ocean that is so energizing for me and my body. She also has the most adorable pets, a Rottweiler called Hunter and a Russian Blue cat called Mali. These two beautiful beings are so joyful to be around. They are always so pleased to see me and are so contributory to me and my body. When I stay the night Mali will come and sleep on the bed next to me.

Who or what do you have in your life that is contributory and you refuse to receive it?

Questions to Empower You

- Am I functioning from contribution or help?
- What contribution am I refusing with my judgements?
- Am I using my assets?
- What would I like to have as my future?

What if?

- What if you were willing to be and receive the contribution of everyone and everything?

- What if you were willing to create your future from ease, joy and glory?

- What if generating and creating was a contribution to the planet?

- What if the future is not anything we thought it was?

If you will do Interesting Point of View I have this point of view" for every point of view that you have, then suddenly you start moving into a place of no context with anything. Total choice, total possibility and total contribution to and from you. Then you can contribute; and when you can contribute, you can be contributed to."

~ Gary Douglas

CHAPTER SIX

This Unchangeable Reality

After looking at the elements of receiving and contribution, we will now be looking at the constructs of this reality and how limitation is created. To have a hedonistic life, you need to break down some of the constructs by which you have been living.

With the unchangeable laws of this reality, all limitations are real and cannot be changed. Have you ever been told that you can't change or do something that you truly desired to change or do?

When I was twenty-four I was choosing to end my first marriage after almost six years. I got married when I had just turned nineteen and I had changed a lot during those years. My first marriage was eighteen months after my mum had died and I chose marriage as a way of escaping from my home life. When I told my dad that I was ending my marriage he was very upset. "You have made your bed, now you must lie in it. Catholics don't get divorced! " These were just a few of his millions of viewpoints. He didn't like change and with these points of view he chose to disown me as his daughter.

The laws of this reality are all about answers or the guru who has your answer, which gives you a conclusion, which gives you a judgement, which gives you a decision, which gives you a computation for the rightness of your conclusion. Are you looking for awareness or for an answer?

The Changeable Laws of Creation

These laws of creation are about question, choice, possibility and contribution. These are the four elements required for your juicy life. If you go to question, you open the door to choices, and then every choice creates an awareness, which creates another set of possibilities. Every possibility opens another door to another question and another choice. Contribution is a two-way street; it's what you gift and how you receive at the same time. It's the simultaneity of gifting and receiving. We misunderstand receiving as being about what we get; however true receiving is getting the energy of what is coming at you and being in awareness, which has no judgement.

This is the shift that is required for you to have a life that is opulent, decadent and orgasmic. If you are looking for the *why* or the answer, you are living in limitation. Don't look for the answer to come to you instantaneously as though by magic. It's a sense of what is possible and waiting until the universe can re-adjust itself. Every time you ask for something different, the universe actually has to adjust itself to give you what you want. If you are working from the changeable laws of creation, because your Titanic has been at the bottom of the ocean for so long, it's going to take a while to get it back up and running in a different direction and away from the iceberg. Just know that it's going to take a little while. Within a year, most of you are going to find that when you ask a question, almost instantaneously, something shows up for you as, "Here, this is what you need to do or where you need to go."

When you are the energy of creation and generation you become the contribution and energy that can change everything on planet earth.

I love being in the energy of nature, watching the waves roll onto the beach and listening to them crashing onto the beach. I love walking through the rainforest. About ten years ago I travelled to New Zealand for the first time to do an Access Consciousness[®]

class with Gary Douglas, the founder. The class opened me up to receive so much more into my life. The day after the class a friend and I hired a car and we travelled all around the North Island. The scenery was astoundingly beautiful, and I had not seen anything like it before. The rainforests meeting the beaches, and everything was all encompassing. It was the oneness—the acoustical vibration. I could hear the trees and the leaves on the trees speaking to me.

It was such a gift to receive that energy. This is what I also have with animals around me. Animals and nature have a certain vibration - an acoustical vibration, which is a similar vibration to classical music. This is the energy of no judgement. Nature and animals don't judge, this is why we love being in this energy. When you are choosing to be the energies of creation and generation, you are being an acoustical vibration. When you choose to function as the acoustical vibration, you are no longer subject to the limitations of this reality. This is when everything becomes easy and effortless. You request of the universe and it shows up. How does it get any better than this?

Now the other side of this is the electrical vibration, which requires you to be in judgement. You cannot maintain electrical vibration without judgement. You are being an electrical vibration when you are having thoughts, feelings and emotions, which is what keeps you trapped in the trauma and drama, upset and intrigue. You need to recognise that by being the acoustical vibration, you can change what is electrical in other people's realities—be yourself and change the world!

There is a hands on the head process in Access Consciousness® called The Bars®. Did you know that there are thirty-two points on your head which when gently touched effortlessly and easily release anything that doesn't allow you to receive? These points contain all the thoughts, ideas, beliefs, emotions and considerations that you have stored in any lifetime. This is an opportunity for you to let go of anything that is no longer working for you. It is an incredibly nurturing and relaxing process, undoing limitation in all aspects of your life that you are willing to change.

How much of your life do you spend doing rather than receiving? Have you noticed that your life is not yet what you would like it to be? You could have everything you desire if you are willing to receive lots more and maybe do a little less. Receiving or learning The Bars® will allow this to begin to show up for you. The Bars® have assisted thousands of people to change many aspects of their body and their life—including sleep, health and weight, money, sex and relationships, anxiety, stress, and so much more. At worst you will feel like you have had a phenomenal massage and at best your whole life can change into something greater with total ease.

A friend of mine who is also a Certified Facilitator and I, taught The Bars® to the inmates in a Brisbane maximum security prison for twelve months. The testimonials from this programme were truly astounding with the inmates stating what had changed for them with total vulnerability. Being the contribution to these men changed my life and my receiving. How did I get so lucky?

Being Energy, Space and Consciousness

Are you now ready to have the elements that are the source for generating new possibilities? If you truly desire to generate something different in your life, you must have the elements of energy, space and consciousness. If you do not have energy and vitality involved in what you are doing, how does anything ever get accomplished? If you do not have the space to be aware of everything, how do you have possibilities? If you have the consciousness to know what is going on and where it's going on, can you generate something different?

Generation is asking the question and being the energetic match. Then whatever has to occur to put that into existence is the construction of it, and you don't necessarily have to be the one to do all of that. Most people believe creation is construction—"I have got to do this and this, in order to get that." Instead, you can ask a question and put the universe to work for you and let it work out the *how*.

In generation you are actually allowing the universe to do a lot of that construction. You just have to ask because generation should be instant rather than this construction that we do. Creation is where you are doing something. "I'm going to create a business" so I have to decide when to do it, where I'm going to do it, what it's going to cost, who's going to come, and who I have to promote to." Does that feel light and fluffy? "Not one little bit," you say. When you are unwilling to be the energy, space and consciousness that generates different possibilities, then you have to function from the reality and the construct of other people's universes. The reality is that you, as a being, are energy, space and consciousness.

When I was getting close to finishing my Naturopathic studies, not only was I studying, I also had full-time employment running the Natural Health section of a large chemist chain where I was living. My kids at the time were still in school, one in high school and one in primary school. With full-time employment I asked the universe for a yummy home to show up for me and my family. It showed up reasonably quickly and so then I started the process of getting a loan to purchase the house. After many knock backs as a female, single income earner with two dependant kids, I made one last attempt and this beautiful female bank manager agreed to do whatever it took to push the loan through. I was so grateful and before I knew it we were moving in.

Then the idea came to me that if I had the house raised and enclosed underneath, I could create a clinic. Talk about a "Field of Dreams"—build it and they will come. And that is exactly what I created. After applying and getting more financing, the builder showed up with ease and within a few months I had a clinic under my living area so I could also work from home and be there for the kids before and after school. I remember the night before the grand opening I was still painting the walls. It was like I was invincible. Nothing or no one was getting in my way to create my dream. There was a demand in my universe for so much more and I knew that the universe had my back. What else is truly possible?

Energy and space are real, and consciousness is the primary material that creates everything. So when you function from energy, space and consciousness instead of matter, energy, space and time, a whole different reality shows up for you because you are generating a life. Time is a linear concept and it is not real, and it is what keeps you locked in the doing and the need to get it right. Your consciousness is the building block for the reality you currently have, so when you are using unconsciousness or anti-consciousness, you are actually *constructing* a life and not *generating* one. Construction is the linear steps you have to follow to put something into existence. This is why if you try to *create* it is actually closer to construction, not generation. "I created this" has no ongoing possibilities; it is over and done. Whereas generation has energy going into it; by virtue of its own continuous generating it is a constant state of new energy. It is not linear because a generative thing goes here, there and everywhere. A creative thing goes in one line. As long as you are functioning from matter, energy, space and time, you are not fully open to receiving because you are locking yourself into the paradigm of the rightness of things as the truth.

Time, dimensions, realities and matter are creations and they are an answer. Energy, space and consciousness are the question and the source of generation. Generation is like what you would have called creation but it has no destruction attached to it. Generation is continuous generation, continuous energy, continuous expansion of possibilities, which is what consciousness is, which is what pure energy is, which is what space is; continuously engendering more space. This is what the generation of you is.

What if functioning from time is a choice? Notice when you think you don't have enough time for something you are always right about that? Yet, when you don't have a point of view about time you've always got more than enough time. You don't suppose time is a creation do you? What if that is a creation that you personally create?

Did time begin the moment you decided it did? Each person creates his or her own time. Time is different for each and every person. Each of us has our own dawn of time. Whenever you started making time relevant in your life was the dawn of time for you personally.

Are you aware that dimension is the idea that something has substance? "This is real" is a reality. "This has substance" is a dimension. Sometimes when you are no longer holding this dimension in existence, you allow yourself to see that you have other creations going on at the same time. That's why it feels like something weird is happening, but you just slipped from one creation to another.

"Reality" is where two or more people align and agree about a point of view. In order to create reality, it requires someone else's alignment and agreement. If you are creating reality you are aligning and agreeing with other people who have no more awareness of what is possible than you do.

As for matter, how often do you make something "matter" and make it significant and therefore make it solid? Notice you have time, dimensions, realities and matter. Is that creation or destruction? Most often it is destruction because you use it to destroy your life and yourself. You can function instead from energy, space and consciousness which will lead to generation.

Now that we have broken down more of the constructs you have been living by, I hope you will have some fun with the generation, creation and institution of a life that is so different that you become the magic. Did you know that the willingness to be present and aware, to be in allowance, is a potency that can change anything? Would you like to know what that is and would you be willing to be the energy of change and possibility?

Questions to Empower You

- Am I looking for awareness or for an answer?
- Am I living from question, choice, possibility and contribution?
- Am I living from the acoustical vibration or the electrical vibration?
- What energy, space and consciousness can I be that would allow me to be the valuable product that I truly BE?
- Am I willing to be the energy of change and possibility?
- What would I like to have as my life and living?

What if?

- What if choosing to be you is a true gift to the planet?
- What if you stopped self-judgement and chose for joy?
- What if you surrendered to your knowing instead of figuring it out?

You are an infinite being; you are energy, space and consciousness. As that you can choose to function from it and generate your life. It is your choice to choose it or not.

   ~ Gary Douglas

CHAPTER SEVEN

Being the Catalyst for Change and Possibility

Do you know what it is to "BE" the catalyst for change and possibility? And what it is to find the elements of your generative life and living?

Every molecule is a generative element unto itself, which is why chemicals put together create different "reactions." So if you are a generative element in the world, you are the catalyst for change and transformation. In life, if you are the catalyst, if you are the chemical that changes everything else then you are that thing that creates a reaction in the world by what you are being.

Are you willing to be the catalyst for change and possibility?

A catalyst is a substance that when added to another substance accelerates a change in it without changing itself. When you are a catalyst for change, the energy and awareness you bring to a situation allows change to occur. The willingness to be present and aware, to be in allowance, is a potency that can change anything. When someone is angry or upset and you are in total allowance of them, you create the space that will allow that person to choose again. That is the potency of life and living; the ability to be the catalyst for the change and transformation of all things and everyone.

We have a catalytic capacity. Literally, by the questions you ask and by the things you do and the words you say, you can transform and change people around you. Have you ever noticed? There are times that by just walking into a room you change the energy of things.

To really start generating your life, you need to act from oneness and consciousness, as it includes everything and judges nothing. It is not about the rightness or wrongness of anything here, it is about the awareness that when you are doing judgement, you are doing limitation. Limitations do not allow the elements of generation, which are actually elegance, aesthetics, decadence, hedonism and liveliness. All judgement destroys all receiving, but if you are doing any of these attributes, then you have no judgement, and from here you can have everything!

So always remember, whether you are aligning and agreeing (which is acceptance), or resisting and reacting to any points of view, thoughts, feelings, emotions, beliefs, judgements, conclusions or considerations you are doing judgement (polarity). Would you like to unlock yourself from the polarity, imprisonment, conditioning and limitation of your thoughts, feelings and emotions? When you choose to live from this space you have little choice and limited possibility. The polarity is what keeps you from actually seeing things as they are so that you can't change what you would like to change. Allowance is where everything is just an interesting point of view and it lets us become aware of all the areas in our life where we are doing judgement.

Discovering Your Generative Energy

So now let's look at some tips for "Discovering Your Generative Energy."

Ask yourself, "What style of life would I like to have?" Not "What would I like to own?"

"What are the elements of the life I would like to live be like? What would the sense of this be?"

If you start from that place you can start to generate what would be joyful to have as your life. But you have to get the parameters of what you would like to create as your life. There's nothing you can't do, there's only things you have decided you don't like to do. When you start your list by listing all the things you don't want to do, what you are creating is "I don't want a life." When you ask for something that brings a sense of joy, you also get peace. You can't have one without the other.

People will ask you, "What do you want to be?" But they are really asking, "What do you want to do?" When you choose what you want to be then you will always know what to do. People do things thinking it creates being. Are you being a chef or are you doing cooking? If you choose being then you are always becoming instead of doing.

Living a Generative Life

So what is "Living a Generative Life" for me? Here are some examples from my list that may assist you with starting your own list.

- ✓ To "Be" me in totality.
- ✓ To have allowance of me and allowance of every choice I make.
- ✓ To have allowance, gratitude, kindness and caring for me and my body.
- ✓ To have the freedom of choice.
- ✓ To "Be" the joy as and with everything.
- ✓ To "Be" flexible, joyful and fit for me and my body.
- ✓ To expand everything that I Be, Do, Have, Create and Generate.

✓ To allow massive amounts of money in my life, and to have ever-expanding financials to 3 million per year and beyond.

✓ To be a phenomenal facilitator and presenter receiving worldwide invitations for expanding conscious awareness.

✓ To travel worldwide three weeks out of every month—and in first class.

✓ To generate my life from hedonism, elegance, decadence, opulence, aesthetics, liveliness and orgasmic living.

✓ To embrace embodiment in every respect for the generative genesis of gracious living.

✓ To meet and work with interesting, fun, joyful and expansive people.

Now, here are some of the elements on my "Not Desired" list of which I have uncreated and destroyed so that I don't have to create them and there is no longer an energetic charge of negativity around them.

✓ Being unhappy, whiny and a victim.

✓ Having poverty—no money, cash and constrained by financial concerns.

✓ Having no home or car.

✓ Being bored with my life

✓ No worldwide or domestic travel.

✓ Having relationships which limit me or my body.

Perhaps this will give you an idea of generating from the energy of who you "BE," and to give you the awareness that it goes far beyond asking for the BMW convertible, or the four-bedroom house with a swimming pool. However, when you "BE" the generative energy, money comes along for the ride. Money always follows fun and joy.

Listen to what you think and say and that will expose all your limitations and everything you can't receive. Ask for the awareness of the energy you might be like, if you were willing to be the energy you can be from that generative space.

What would that energy be like? Look at the energy of what your life would be like if you were being the energy you would like to be at all times; not what you think it ought to come out like based on a result.

Ask: "If I were generating my life, what would the sense of that be?" There is no resulting point of view in that question. It's not what it would look like; it's what it would BE like. What would I like to accomplish?

If you can truly get that generation is like being a battery, an electrical current, a never-ending supply of energy that is constantly flowing, while creation is more like a light switch; it's either on or it's off. Creation requires it's polar opposite which is destruction. Generation does not have any polarity in it. If you are generating your life, it is a constant flow, a constant increase and there is no completion. Does energy ever complete? Do atoms and molecules complete? Or do they continue to generate and transform?

Have you been taught to finish things, to mark your life by your accomplishments and successes? To stay in your job until retirement and then collect your gold watch? These are the reference points you use to determine if you are having a life but the completion point of life is death.

What if accomplishment was the beginning of something greater? What if there was no completion? What if everything you complete is a contribution to the next thing you can create or generate? Would that continually expand your life? When you say, "I've completed this. Cross it off the list!" you go into the destruct cycle of creation. Instead of going to destruct, ask, "What can I create and generate now that is even greater?" How many people do you know who have a "Bucket List" from which they scratch off what they have completed?

Questions to Empower You

- If I were generating my life, what would the sense of that be?
- What would I like to accomplish?
- What would I like to have as my life and living?

What if?

- What if everything I complete is a contribution to the next thing I can create or generate?
- What if there was no completion?
- What if accomplishment was the beginning of something greater?

Know that from everything you have already done, you have altered your awareness to embrace the possibility of something more. You haven't completed, you have contributed to a new possibility. Everything you are willing to contribute to and be part of creates a different reality. That's oneness.

~ Gary Douglas

CHAPTER EIGHT

Purpose and Priorities

Another element to be aware of that stops the generative energies is "Purpose." Have you been driven to "Find Your Purpose?"

For many years I was driven to find my life's' purpose. Dan Millman's book *Finding Your Life Purpose* was my bible. I read it in any spare moment that I had, as I was obsessed with finding my life purpose. Of course it didn't help that I was doing a lot of personal development programmes at the time and I was buying into their point of view that I was not on track with my life whilst I didn't have a life purpose. I started to realise that I was making myself so wrong so I chose to let it go and started to have more fun in my life. And the more fun that I was having the more fun my life became. That was much lighter for me than constantly searching for my life purpose.

Soon after that I was invited to attend a "Women in Business" lunch meeting. This was a group of women from all walks of life who got together monthly to network and have some fun. Arriving late, a woman sat in the spare chair beside me and took total control of the conversation by announcing that she was a business coach and that she was late because she was working with clients to change the world and how important her job was, and that she had found her purpose. After some time and making the conversation all about her, she turned to me and with total disdain asked me; "So what is your life purpose and what are you doing to change the planet?" I responded with, "Having fun!" She then said, "So, how is that going to change the planet?" "Well, I said, I figure that if everyone is having fun, it would be a planet of peace, abundance and joy." At that, she got up from her chair and walked away. Perhaps that was very controversial for her.

The generative energy here is priority not purpose. There is a big distinction between purpose and priority and it affects everything in your life. Purpose is what we use to achieve and accomplish everything and you also use it to constantly judge whether you are doing it right or doing enough.

Priority is what you use to create possibility. If it's a priority it's just there and it's a creative and generative possibility and it leads you but it's not something you ever have to judge. A priority is something you can always choose more of. You will always be seeking approval when you have purpose, whereas priority just gives us choice.

For me writing this book is a priority, not a purpose. I am choosing to be creative and generative with the possibilities of creating a greater future. Priorities are required if you wish to create a future. When I have a priority I will choose differently instead of falling through life and falling into my future. A priority is the choice I would make before I make another choice. Priority is a source for creation. I don't have to succeed at my priority, I just choose again. If no one ever chooses to purchase or read this book that is OK because I am having fun creating it and I am choosing my life from the fun and joy.

**Purposes will eliminate every future
you could create.**

What Are Purposes?

Purpose always requires decisions, judgements and conclusions, which are all limitations. There is no question with purpose. It is the need to have the right answer. Having a purpose eliminates choice. Having a purpose is the idea that you must judge whether you have succeeded or not.

How many purposes do you have as the source of your life? How many purposes are you engaged in that keep you locked in judgement and away from generating and creating?

Purpose is designed to create and maintain your judgement of you. Are you actualising what your judgements are of you? If there were no reasons for doing anything, what would you do, that you are currently not doing?

What Are Priorities?

Priority requires question, choice, possibility and contribution. *What is my priority today?* Asking this question is about recognizing what is a priority in your life and getting clear on that for yourself. Would you be willing to be brutally honest with what is true for you? Everything gets easier from that honesty with self. When you get clear on what is really your priority, you will create it easily. Priority is the willingness to shift and change all the time to have something greater show up.

If you have a purpose to "make a difference in people's lives" then do you have to judge you if it doesn't happen? Absolutely! If you have a purpose as a facilitator of change to bring people to consciousness, do you judge the people who don't choose consciousness or do you just judge yourself? You will judge you as not enough, or not right enough if you have a purpose.

Can you get the difference of energies of priority and purpose? Having a priority to "make a difference" is totally different. You always have choice to make this your priority and you don't have to choose it all the time, everyday, and you don't ever have to judge yourself whether you achieve it or not. You just get to show up as you in that moment, and not have any points of view of you.

What Are Assigns and Assignations?

Assigns are the issues that have been given to you as your problem or your difficulty. Have you ever said, "I have a money issue or I have a fear issue?" Issue means something that has been given to you, not something that you chose.

The assignations are where the assigns come together with this reality and lock you up as though it's true. What if nothing was real or true? What would you have available to you? Would you have total choice?

Did you have parents who put on you that you need to be or do or create your life in a certain way? I know I did.

When I was in Year 10 of high school and looking at my choices for higher education as I was choosing to go on to university, my dad and I attended a parent/teacher interview. At the time my mum was too ill to attend. When I expressed my plan to attend university, my dad interjected with, "Get that nonsense out of your head. You are female and you will just get married and have a family. There is no money for an education, and if there was it would just be wasted." How is that for fixed points of view and limitations?

After Year 10 finished, I won a scholarship to a technical college. When looking at the choices, I became disgruntled as there was nothing on the list that interested me. I closed my eyes and with the point of a pen I picked a course. It was "Dress Designing." This was a three year course, and so this was the beginning of the next chapter of my life. This course held very little interest for me, so the next two years was spent mostly in the coffee shop smoking cigarettes and drinking coffee. Needless to say, my results from the exams weren't great. At the end of the second year my mum died, so I didn't return to college, however I knew that I had to make another choice. One day I walked into one of Brisbane's top bridal wear stores and asked for a job. Within a week I started work there designing and making bridal and formal wear. This led me into making costumes for the Queensland Opera, Theatre, and Ballet Companies. Eventually I started my own businesses and I had a lot of fun along the way. It is only now that I can acknowledge that I have lived from the "What else can I add to my life?"

You have been told forever that you need to have a higher purpose which makes you want to follow someone who you believe has more awareness than you. When you do priority you are accused of being selfish because priorities are not about a higher purpose. Priorities are about awareness.

You can't have a purpose to have fun, but you can have a priority to have fun.

Actualisation

Actualisation is what you can bring into existence which is a creative and generative energy. Your physical actualisation is your creative generative capacity. If what you are actualising is not what you desire, you may have a purpose there. Ask yourself:

What purpose do I have here that is creating this and what priority can I choose that would change this? Would consciousness change this?

What if your priority is to be free to choose anything? By giving up your purpose for something, you gain access to your priority.

Do you have a purpose not to make a mistake? To fight everyone including you? Were you told your life would work if you got smart enough? What if your priority is always to go beyond your own limitations and always being willing to see what your limitations are? Then you will always be in question.

Are you willing to continue to ask and choose differently in order to create your future?

For me right now more than at any other time in my life, everything that I have decided is real is breaking and falling apart. A month or so ago I did an advanced Access Consciousness® class with Gary Douglas and Dain Heer. Since then the sense of everything breaking and falling apart has been intense. I have to stay as in the question of "Is everything really falling apart or falling together?" What if now is the time to create from a totally different space? Am I willing to have that? Is this the opportunity for me to go into creation?

The three choices that we have in life are: generation, creation and institution. Generation is the energy of something you would like to bring into existence or actualize. Creation is what you have to do to bring it into actualization. Institution is the maintenance program. Is your life a maintenance programme? Do you get up in the morning and ask, "What grand and glorious adventure and true magic can I be, do, have, create and generate today?" Or do you get up and go, "What do I have to do today?" Do you have a to-do list that you are using to limit you and take you away from following the energy?

Questions to Empower You

- Am I using "Purpose" to create achievement and accomplishment?

- What purpose do I have here that is creating this and what priority can I choose that would change this?

- How many purposes do I have that lock up and limit everything I would like to change in my life?

- What is my priority today?

- Am I being brutally honest with myself today?

- What priorities are you unwilling to choose, that if you chose them would make your life everything you want it to be?

- How many purposes do I have creating *(this limitation)* and what priorities could I have?

- Is this a purpose or a priority? Am I using a purpose here or choosing a priority?

What if?

- What if there were no reasons for doing anything, what would you do, that you are currently not doing?

- What if your priority is to have fun?

- What if your priority is to be free to choose anything?

- What if your priority is always to go beyond your own limitations and always being willing to see what your limitations are?

- What if what you think is your purpose is actually a priority and you have never acknowledged it?

- What purpose do I have here that is creating this and what priority can I choose that would change this?

Assigns and assignations are what you give yourself to make yourself right in this reality; you have given yourself these assigns and assignations of what your purpose is. Is your purpose to always be right?

~ Gary Douglas

CHAPTER NINE

The Lie of Cause and Effect

What if cause and effect are the ultimate lie of this reality? You can change anything if you *choose,* but you have to choose to change it. What you believe is that you can't change or get free of anything unless you find the cause of it so you can be free of the effect of it. Are you looking for *why* something is happening, trying to find the "cause" for the "effect"? What if instead of looking for and asking the question, "What's causing this?" you might ask, "What can I change here?" We all have been taught that we are either the cause or the effect in life. Cause and effect always makes you wrong whether you are the cause (you are the source point) or the effect (the victim). It is a justification and it eliminates creativity and all power and potency to create or generate change.

How much of your life is being driven by cause and effect? What would your life be without it?

Recently a client of mine was accused of saying lots of things that were mean and judgemental about others. Firstly, please always remember, when someone is accusing you of something, that is because that is where they are functioning from. When someone accuses you of doing competition that is because they are doing competition as an example. When they accuse you of saying mean and judgemental things about others that is what they are doing. At first, my friend got really angry and when anger shows up there may be lies there that make you angry. A lie will always make you angry. So I asked him if there were lies that were making him angry and he said that he got a "yes". This question made him have a sense of lightness. I asked him, "What is the truth here and what are the lies, spoken or unspoken?" I cleared the energy of everything that came up from asking this and then asked him the following questions: "What is this? What do you do with it? Can you change it? If so how do you change it? What is this person choosing to create here?"

In asking lots of questions he got to have a deeper awareness that empowered him to know what was going on for this person. It was then that he realised that the person who was accusing him was in the pain of self-judgement and of not creating and generating their life of choice. All of that energy was being projected onto him and he was being blamed for them not creating more. He chose to be empowered by this event, and he is very aware that it would have been very easy to be at the effect of their choices. Choosing to be the victim no longer works for him. *How does it get any better than this?*

When we come from the space of being who we are, we are aware of the gift of magnificence that we truly be. What if all judgement, hatred, jealousy and fear stem from people not realizing their true greatness?

Were you ever encouraged to express who you truly are? If we all were, would we be loving beings, each bringing our uniqueness to the world? How much judgement have we created about what is perfect, which leads to doubt and competitiveness? Perfection is the positive polarity, which is judgement.

What if what is showing up in the world isn't from the judgement and hatred we have for others but for ourselves?

If I make a choice which creates a potential (I'm going to this cooking class) but if I then follow that up with a fixed point of view about that potential (I know all about cooking already), no new reality can be created. If you follow up with a question like, "What can I learn here?" then that creates a new reality. As soon as a new reality is created we tend to go to, "What caused this change?" instead of asking another question like, "What else is possible? What choices do I have that could change this?"

A few years ago I fractured and dislocated my knee. I was driving myself crazy looking for the cause of the fall—was I distracted, and not being present with my body, or was it the glasses of wine I had had earlier, all of which was making me the effect of my choices. The belief is that if I could find the cause then I could change or remove the effect, the pain in my body. Does that really work? It didn't for me.

What I started to do instead was ask, "What energy does my body require? What energy can I run through my body that will create a change here?" And then I did that and many of my friends turned up to assist me with that also. I didn't know what "effect" that was going to create, I just knew that something would change by my choice to ask for change.

"How did I cause this effect?" is not a question. It's a conclusion with a question mark attached. You have decided you must have done something to create what is showing up so you can't change it until you find the cause, which puts you at the effect. Is this the lie that traps you? Every conclusion, every limitation, every disease is a choice you have made.

You are the potency for change and generation. There is no cause and effect, only choice, question and change. Choice is not cause, it's just choice. Your choices are the source for generation which is not cause. "Cause" is fixed; choice is generated in every second.

You look for the choice which will generate the effect you would like to create. That's not choice. When you don't function from cause and effect you can generate absolutely anything. You can just choose to change something. You can affect the world; you are not an effect on the world.

Affect means to influence to action or to move. Effect is a result or consequence of something. So you can create change by affecting something. Effect implies no choice and being victim to a cause. When you feel someone has put you in the "effect" position, you have to fight them to get into the "cause" position, but you are still at the effect of the cause and effect point of view.

Awareness Is Not Cause and Effect

A question is what's required to reveal an awareness of choices. When you ask questions like, "What is it?" from a place of looking for a cause, then you become the effect. When you ask, "What is it?" from space, you are asking, "What can I be, do, have, create or generate that can change this?" "This is the way it works," is not cause and effect; it's awareness. People think if they get more aware then this "effect" won't happen again.

What would your life be like without cause and effect?

When you step out of cause and effect, there is no more "How do I do this?" or "I have to do this" in your Universe. It's just, "This is what I want. What's it going to take to get it?" Then what you have available to you is not the energy to force you into having to do something, but instead, "What would I like to do today?" It is no longer about, "How do I do this?" but instead, "What do I need to do today to create, generate and institute this?"

There will be no reason to live just a choice in every new moment. If you choose to live in every present moment, then you will have a joyful life and living. If you require the reasons to live, then everything is predicated on someone else's point of view. There is no reason to live. Do the birds have a reason to sing? Do the fruit trees have a reason to create fruit? Or do they just do it? Are you looking for a reason to live? Do you have reasons to live? What if you were as simple as a tree or a bird? What if you did nothing unless it was fun for you? The cause and effect universe is not real. Are you making it important when it doesn't have to be?

Questions to Empower You

- What can I change here?
- What else is possible?
- What choices do I have that could change this?
- What is this?
- What questions can I ask?
- What possibilities are here?
- What would my life be like without cause and effect?

What if?

- What if you knew you were not at the effect of anyone or anything?
- What if you knew that you were not the shopping trolley of the world for every opinion that is delivered at you?
- What if you were aware of your true value?
- What if you are way more potent than you think you are?
- What if cause and effect are the ultimate lie?

Awareness is not in the cause and effect universe. Functioning from cause and effect eliminates the capacity to see the future. Using a question to create a space for receiving creates a greater possibility than pushing for a cause to create a specific effect.

~ Gary Douglas

CHAPTER TEN

What Are Quantum Entanglements?

"Quantum entanglement," in simple terms, is when two objects are linked in such a way that when you interact with one it instantaneously resonates with the other.

That is, a molecule here may have a resonance with a molecule in another time, location, dimension or reality.

It's the difference between how you do or don't generate or create.

Every point of view has a molecular structure so whatever you have held onto as valuable will create itself again in the future so you have the same molecular structure there. For instance, if your point of view is "I am not creating" those molecules transfer to the future and create the molecules of "I am not creating"; the future shows up as you being "no creation" as you have decided you are. Every point of view you create changes your future and maintains the limitation of your reality.

The choice of your point of view is what creates the future. A fixed point of view travels into the future as a *quantum entanglement*. An "interesting" point of view does not create this because it is not fixed so it can't resonate into the future. If you destroy your point of view, you are destroying the charge, but you still have to be in "interesting" point of view and choose a different reality in order not to recreate it.

Using Quantum Entanglements for Creation

Quantum entanglements create the string theory of time. The string theory is the idea that all things are connected and if you follow the string you will see how all things are interrelated.

When you have a thought, it entangles with other people's thoughts, and in so doing creates a reality in which all realities lock in together as the same reality. All things are inter-related. Nothing is separate by itself.

Quantum entanglements are the agreed-upon points of view that people have used to create their limitations and their possibilities. Quantum entanglements don't just deal with the past. They deal with the present and the future as well. They deal with everything, including other people's points of view and how the future is being created by people's points of view.

For example, If you create doubt in your awareness, your requirement for doubt pulls in all the doubt of everyone else all over the universe in order to solidify your doubt into existence. The quantum entanglements support you to maintain everything you are asking for.

Quantum entanglements are particles we throw into the future to create more limitation like we have now. You use the electrical component of the molecules to impel the particle into the future – there is no choice or possibility.

When you ask for quantum entanglements, you are asking for the consciousness that exists in all things, not just the people. Every molecule has consciousness. Every molecule will support you. But if you don't get how the quantum entanglements of the molecular structure of all things in the universe are willing to contribute to you, then you can't totally receive.

For some time now I have been running the following process that you can use, or create one that works for you to request what you would like of the quantum entanglements.

Ask yourself: What generative capacity for instant generation of the elementals into solidification by request of the quantum entanglements, fulfilled as living with care, kindness, gratitude, joy, peace, possibility, gentleness and lightness of being for me and my body do I have that I am not inviting as living?

I spoke in Chapter Eight about everything that I have known as real breaking and falling apart. That is particularly this case   in regards to running this process. It's like everything that shows up in my life demands of me and my body to have the energy of care, kindness, gratitude, joy, peace, possibility, gentleness and lightness of being. It is amazing knowing that the quantum entanglements are bringing me everything that I have asked for. I am so grateful.

When you are willing to ask for these things to come into existence, you are actually changing reality by your request. When you ask for the quantum entanglements to become fulfilled as what you would like, you are working towards creating the future you would like to have.

If you ask the molecular structure of all things in the universe to contribute to you, they will. This is making something solid by your perceiving, knowing, being and receiving of the acoustical vibrations—not from thoughts, feelings and emotions. Request and then be willing to wait.

What Are the Elementals?

The dictionary describes elementals as the pure essence or basic form of things. Specifically, the definition reads: 1. fundamental;

basic; primal: *the elemental needs of man* 2. motivated by or symbolic of primitive and powerful natural forces or passions: *elemental rites of worship* 3. of or relating to earth, air, water, and fire considered as elements 4. of or relating to atmospheric forces, esp. wind, rain, and cold 5. of, relating to, or denoting a chemical element).

Elementals are the basis of the construction of realities; the molecules. The basic elements for the construct of reality are energy, space and consciousness.

Elementals are the molecular structures that exist in all realities. Are you refusing to create and institute these things in order to keep this reality as it is? This is how you allow your reality to be out of existence in favour of somebody else's point of view.

If you solidify energy, space and consciousness—the elementals— into reality, you create a different reality.

Can you now see that thoughts, feelings, emotions, beliefs, need and greed are not solid? Everything you think is badness, everything you judge, is what you are solidifying into reality. You are trying to avoid destruction as though that is creation and it isn't.

Solidification of the elementals is asking the molecular structure of all things to contribute and become what you have asked for. It is the beginning of creation (not manifestation or actualisation). It is at this point that all things in the world start to adjust themselves to make things come to fruition for you. This is a form of creation that you have never engaged in. The elementals are the essence of the plants, and the weather and the acoustical vibration of the world is made solid by these. It's every acoustical vibration that exists. It's a musical universe where the trees are clapping and the flowers are singing. If you would embrace that, would your life and living be total ease?

This is beyond magic. This is creating your life. Creationism is creating your life, not trying to undo what doesn't work. Ask for what you would like to show up and not for the awareness of how you are unable to do something.

You don't realise that by every choice you make, you are actually placing a request on the universe for what it will deliver for you. So when you have upset, trauma and drama, the quantum entanglements that are dedicated to upset, trauma and drama will support creating more upset and intrigue in order to fulfil your request.

I have had many clients who are destroying their lives with trauma and drama. Over the years I have heard the same statements over and over. "How come all of the bad stuff keeps happening to me?" It is like "Groundhog Day" for many of them. Usually what I say is, "Same shit, different day." So really what is showing up or being created here is that they are requesting the quantum entanglements to give them more of the abuse, trauma, drama or whatever else it is that they are asking for. How easy would this be to change if more people had this information? How empowering would it be for people to know that by asking a question and making new choices everything would change? Would the need for drugs, psychiatrists and other insanities disappear?

If you make anything more solid and real rather than going, "OK, what choice do I have here?" the quantum entanglements will make it solid and real for you—however you want it. You are creating with the quantum entanglements now, but it's not necessarily what you'd like.

With the quantum entanglements, if you are dealing with a person who is funky around money, and you try to keep them from being funky, you have already bought into it, so you have increased their funkiness for them with the quantum entanglements. If you request of the quantum entanglements to create space around an issue, they will create space around the issue. Then the other person can't get funky even if they want to, because there are not enough quantum entanglements supporting the funk.

Using the Quantum Entanglements Against You

How much of the "bad things" in your life are showing up because your way of requesting is, "I hate this?" So the quantum entanglements dedicated to the hate throughout the world join forces to help you get exactly what you hate. Going into question allows a different reality to show up.

If you say, "I am sick and tired," then the quantum entanglements have to create you getting sick and tired. Then the only reason your body gets sick and tired is because that's what you were asking for. If you say, "I am sick and tired," all the quantum entanglements designed to create sickness and tiredness must support you in what you have requested. That's how it impacts your body. Please don't do that. You have decided it impacts your body and then you state it after the fact. You have already taken the point of view that it sickens and tires you. Is this really what you want to create?

If you go, "I don't have enough money," the quantum entanglements create more of having not enough money. Instead, what if you asked, "What would it take for me to have too much money?" Remember when I asked that question, a $10,000 diamond ring showed up in my life.

Are you willing to trust that your creative and generative capacities are capable of creating a greater world?

If you refuse to request of the quantum entanglements, it's a way to make sure that you never have to become the source for creating a different reality.

Would you be willing to make the request of the quantum entanglements to create what you truly desire in life? Are you refusing to have the generation, creation and institution of what is actually possible? Are you always looking to have something that fits this reality rather than creating your reality totally?

Are you willing to have a reality that is so different from everybody else's that you can stand alone, all by yourself, and have no point of view? Are you willing to be aware of this generative capacity you have to solidify things into existence?

Are you willing to be part of the oneness that actually is the generative energy for all other realities? Or would you rather go along with what everybody else has chosen? That is the way you entrain yourself, rather than being willing to actually be fulfilled totally as a different reality, knowing that you as a different reality can generate, create and institute a totally different possibility in the world.

Are you willing to have more possibilities? You do have a choice. You can try and live in this reality, or you can create one in which you get everything you ever wanted and more.

In order to have everything the quantum entanglements offer you, you have to have something that has not ever been on this planet, which is a cohesiveness of being and receiving. We have tried to create being and receiving as separate things. *The reality is, you cannot receive unless you can be.* You have to be and receive simultaneously for everything to come to fruition with ease.

Questions to Empower You

- What capacity for instant generation of the elementals into solidification by request of the quantum entanglements fulfilled as the joy of living do you have that you are not inviting?

- What generative capacity for instant generation of the elementals into solidification by request of the quantum entanglements fulfilled as the joy of living with care, kindness, gratitude, peace and possibility for me do I have that I am not inviting as living?

- Would I rather go along with what everybody else has chosen? Am I willing to choose from rewarding choice?

- What can I be that would alter this, change this, and create a different reality?

What if?

- What if requesting of the quantum entanglements gave you everything that you are asking for?

- What if requesting of the quantum entanglements is what is required to change everything that is not working for you?

If you are willing to receive everything, the quantum entanglements will give you every piece of information you need to handle everything in your life at any moment. If you are not willing to totally receive, then you will reject what would allow you to change anything that occurs.

~ Gary Douglas

CHAPTER ELEVEN

Choosing from the Kingdom of We

The kingdom of "we" is the kingdom of consciousness and oneness. When you are functioning from the kingdom of "we," you are asking for everything to be easier for you, and "you" includes *everybody* around you.

This is living by choice, not by automatic pilot. Automatic pilot is not creating from awareness. When you function from the kingdom of "we," you choose what works for you *and* everybody else —but you do not have to choose against someone else in order to choose for you. You don't eliminate what you require and desire in the choices you make. When you make the choices that include you and everybody else, it is always an expanding of your agenda. You being you is what is necessary in order to create the kingdom of we; you don't exclude yourself in any interaction and you don't exclude others either. You are being present for people. It's a totally different energy and people are amazed by that. It is the difference between being and beingness.

Beingness is going to a store and talking loudly about yourself to the salesperson and spending lots of money so people will notice and remember you. That is doing (spending money) to be.

Being, on the other hand, is including the salesperson in the transaction and acknowledging them and allowing them to contribute to you. That salesperson will remember your gratitude and acknowledgement no matter how much you spend.

Many people just naturally desire to gift but they are never given a chance because they are never received. When you function from the kingdom of "we," you open up this place where others can gift and actually be received. As a result, instead of people taking advantage of you, they will actually desire to gift you more.

Choosing from the Kingdom of Me

People who are stuck in the kingdom of "me" are trying to encapsulate themselves to give themselves a sense of safety. The kingdom of me means you're not aware of anybody outside of you. There are people who live in that place of encapsulating and separating as a way of creating a refuge in their life. Many people who get into horses use the horse as a way of encapsulating themselves. The only place they feel "safe" is with their animal. They are looking for that refuge—that place of not having to be involved with other people.

You are on a planet in which involvement with other people is a necessity. If you function from the kingdom of "we," you have to have the awareness of what somebody can receive and be, and then you are also aware of the judgement they have of you and how to deal with it. Then you have greater control over them than they have over you. In the kingdom of we, it's about how you gain control over your life and everybody else's.

However, if you reside in the kingdom of *me,* you are always shutting out your awareness of what may contribute to your life in some way that could be quite dynamic.

In the kingdom of *me* you give up your position for somebody else. In the kingdom of *we,* no one has to give up anything. Everybody gets to be exactly who they are and choose as they choose. You get to be aware of what they are choosing and you don't try to give you up in order to get what they want to choose.

Have you given up your awareness, your intelligence, and your knowing in order to create a relationship – friendship or otherwise? You give up all of that so the other person won't judge you, except they have already judged you.

Most of us have been trying to choose for ourselves our whole life, thinking that, "if I can choose for me, then I will finally get it." But when you are choosing from the kingdom of me, you are the first person that gets eliminated in the choices you make.

How much of choosing for you has always been, "I'll just give them what they want?" That's the kingdom of me. "How is this going to work for me *as well as them?*" is the kingdom of we. When you start to function from the kingdom of we, you include you. As long as you are doing the kingdom of me, you exclude you. The "me" is always the exclusion, never the truth or the possibility.

You destroy you when you don't include yourself in the computation of your own life. When someone requires of you that you spend time with them, if that's not part of your platform, it becomes an irritant. It's like having a needy child who doesn't want you to leave home. You need to look at what's true for you. If you are a person who likes your alone time, then you have to enjoy the fact that you have your alone time and not think there is anything wrong with it, because alone time is what works for you. Some people can't stand being alone. Some people do not wish to know themselves at all.

When I got divorced for the second time almost thirty years ago, I realised how much I enjoyed my alone time. Even though I had the kids full time, after their bedtime, the alone time was so empowering for me. The peace and space was so rewarding and nurturing. I haven't chosen to do traditional relationship and marriage from this reality's points of view ever since. I certainly don't judge it as wrong as many others do. I very much enjoy male company and choose it when and how it works for me. I am so grateful that I was willing to see that doing relationships the way that others do it never worked for me. As I choose to create the connection and communion with myself, if someone amazing shows up who also chooses so much more, I will never close the door on the "What else is possible?"

I see people I know jumping from one relationship and marriage to the next, divorcing and destroying themselves in the process. Are they looking to find themselves in the other person? *What if you were willing to be you, regardless of who is in your life?*

I am no longer willing to divorce and destroy myself to have a relationship with anyone.

Have you ever been accused of being selfish, self-centred, and self-serving? What if all of that is a lie? You have never, in your entire life, been selfish—even when you tried to be. Have you ever been able to choose from a self-serving point of view? If you did, did you go into judgement of you?

Kingdom of me is the answer for how to satisfy other people's needs. Kingdom of we raises these questions: "What choices do I have here? What will expand my agenda and create a greater possibility?"

Every choice you make isn't about just including yourself, it includes everybody else. Do you desire greater consciousness? You can't make a choice that creates consciousness for yourself and not for everybody else. Do you know that you are not alone?

Oneness Includes Everything and Judges Nothing

The kingdom of we is the quantum entanglements brought into existence in a totally different reality. It's a choice you have to make. When you start to see the quantum entanglements from another place, you start to realise it's not a concept. It's a reality.

Questions to Empower You

- What question can I ask or be here that would create a different possibility?

- What's my priority here?

- What would I really like to create as my life?

- What else is possible?

- What else can I do or be?

- What else can I create and generate?

- What else would be fun for me?

What if?

- What if choosing to function from the kingdom of we creates a space of change and possibility?

- What if being selfish, self-centred and self-serving is all a lie?

Kingdom of we includes question, choice, possibility and contribution. Kingdom of me is always about coming to the right conclusion, the right answer and the right justification. It is being an expert, rather than: "What question will change and expand everything?"

~ Gary Douglas

CHAPTER TWELVE

Planning Your Future, Goals and Targets

The dictionary definition of goal is "The final purpose or aim; the end to which a design tends, or which a person aims to reach or attain."

Many of the coaching, personal and professional development programmes that I have participated in the past 30 or so years have required me to write my goals. Whenever we got to this section of the course, the resistance and hesitancy would come up for me big time. I have always struggled with getting clear about what my goals were, and it was always easy to judge myself because others appeared to have no problems with writing their goals. When I realised that the meaning of the word was about final purpose or aim, which is all limitation, then I was grateful that for me it was about the question "What else is possible?" rather than the conclusion and end result.

Do you judge yourself when you don't achieve your goals? What if having targets that you got to shoot at over and over if you missed the bullseye the first time, was a rewarding choice for you?

Are you now ready to clear away the solidification of the past in favour of the possibility of a future?

Have you been trying to solidify your future into existence by deciding, judging, or determining something? Most people determine their lives based on their plans, their goals and their map of the future that they think they want to have. Have you had any idea what "mapping out your future" meant? Many people have an intense map! They plan what they are going to have in their future and then they start figuring out how to get it.

I know this young couple who have the next few years planned out almost down to the day. The solidity of this planning leaves no room for the "What else is possible?"

The conclusion, decisions and judgements that it takes to keep it all in existence is massive. It is like forcing everything into existence, instead of creating from question, choice, possibility and contribution—which is where the magic lives.

I love the magic that shows up when I am in question, choice, possibility and contribution. A friend of mine who I had been coaching was incredibly grateful for the changes that I had facilitated him to. In gratitude, he invited me to dinner at a very decadent and opulent restaurant. During that day I became aware that he was also celebrating his birthday even though he hadn't mentioned that to me. I started asking questions in regards to how I could surprise him for his birthday. What would it take to have something yummy for him as a surprise for dessert? I looked at buying a cake or baking one and taking it with me, except that it wouldn't be a surprise for long as he was picking me up. "What are the possibilities of the chef making a phenomenal desert for him?" I asked. Before I knew it he was at my doorstep to pick me up and I still hadn't organised anything with the restaurant. "No worries, I thought, I will talk to the chef when I get there". When we arrived my friend had organised a bottle of French champagne and some delicious tapas for us to enjoy and celebrate whilst we ordered our meal. I was so in the moment of the delicious champagne and food dancing on my tastebuds that I totally forgot about the birthday dessert.

We were ushered to our table, where to my body's delight, was the most scrumptious looking hot and cold seafood platter. We were savouring every mouthful whilst laughing and enjoying every moment with sheer delight. When the waiter came to clear the table and to ask if we would like dessert, I realised that I still hadn't spoken to the chef. In that moment I chose to let it go. I totally let go of the point of view that I had to surprise him for his birthday. Perhaps this evening was about me receiving the gratitude that he had for me.

My friend ordered a plate consisting of different flavoured gelato ice cream.

When the waiter arrived to serve the gelato, he wished my friend a happy birthday. With a surprise on his face, my friend asked the waiter, "How do you know it is my birthday?" The waiter pointed to the plate and answered, "It has Happy Birthday written across the top of the plate."

How was that possible, I hear you ask? Is it possible that I put the thought into the chef's head and he was willing to psychically pick it up? I love the magic, and I am always asking for it. What would it take to have the magic of living?

Do you have the point of view that accomplishment is the target for the creation of future?

Do you have the point of view that if you don't have a future plan, you can't have a future? Every time you create a target, then you know you're going for that. As long as you're going towards that, even if you haven't achieved it, you still believe in a future. Once you have achieved all those things, you assume it's time to retire or give up. Those are also all projected future realities. Are you creating your goals and targets as the purpose of living? Whilst you are shooting for that, do you think you have a purpose? Does this give you a reason for living, or to get the life that is "right"?

The problem with all of this is that the goals are all predicated on this reality. That is why so many people have difficulty when a change occurs. The change is so disruptive that they lose their goal and their motivation and suddenly they don't know what to do. They have lost their reason and justification for living.

Most people come to conclusion about what their target is supposed to be, what they are supposed to have, and what's right. So they limit everything in their lives based on that, based on this reality. What if there was a different reality available that you have never seen?

Have you been trying to create from this reality in terms of how you are supposed to create your future and your reality based on having a target, going after it, achieving it and that creates a rung on your ladder of success? Does that really mean anything to you? What if you have a desire to have total awareness, no matter what it looks like?

Would you be willing to have this reality work for you instead of you working in this reality?

What if you were willing to ask; "What would I like my reality to be? Where could I function from?"

Having a Platform

When you have your platform, you are not trying to create from a goal or a target, nor are you trying to create a life based on your map. You are trying to create something that is a platform from which the rest of your life could be built. If you can get some clarity on what your personal platform is, then everything will start to function from that and start to move forward because you have given the universe the platform off of which you wish to build a different reality.

Usually you can tell what your platform is by a time in your life when you were totally enjoying it. When you have elements of your platform in place, money may not be totally abundant, but it isn't a problem or a difficulty either. Your platform is what makes anything possible in your life and creates the enthusiasm you would like to have in your life that you currently don't have. It doesn't matter what your platform is. It only matters that you have a platform and that you're aware that your platform gives you choices.

A platform is something from which you can build more. When you have a platform from which you build something, if there is a change, the platform doesn't change, but the structure of what you are building can change. Your platform still carries you, regardless of the situation. Your platform should be that which allows you to be you and create and generate everything based on that. A foundation is a definition of what can be in existence, so rather than a foundation, build a platform for your life.

Without a platform you are floundering. Once you have a platform, you know what you are standing on, and there is no longer that sense that you are in quicksand. How much of your life have you been creating as though you are in quicksand, trying to get out, trying to create the target that will allow you to pull yourself out of something, rather than asking what you would like to catapult yourself into. Your platform is a springboard for what your life can be. You are the energy of your platform.

Finding Your Platform

Are you aware of what creates enthusiasm in your own life about living? To find your platform, think back to a time in your life when you had a sense of joy and possibility and you never thought about money, but money just showed up in weird ways for you at that time. Think about when you had a creative generative ease with being. That's when you're functioning from the platform of your life. What are the elements that you had then that you are missing now in your life? Those elements are part of your platform.

Are you looking for the platform that will make you money? Trying to build a platform based on money will not work. Easy money is not about the amount, it's when it came easy and you didn't have to think about it, where you enjoyed what you were doing so much that it wasn't about the money. You have undoubtedly had some place in your life where that existed.

Several months before I moved back to Brisbane, I was there doing a course and visiting friends. One of my friends invited me to join him for a coffee. He was telling me about this "Money Game" that he had been introduced to and was I interested in joining him. He scribbled some figures on the back of a coaster and asked me if I was in. Sure, I said, why not. Even though I had no clue what he was going on about, it had such a fun energy to it. He looked at me and asked for $2,000. Without hesitation, I opened my wallet and handed him the cash. A week later after I had arrived home, he rang me to inform me that I was about to collect $16,000, however I had not invited two additional people to play the game. I informed him that I lived in a country town that thrived on lack and scarcity, and I wasn't aware of anyone who had a spare $2,000 to throw at a game. At that he suggested that he would put in $2,000 and if I did the same that would make me qualify. The whole thing was surreal to me. I did what was required and three days later, $16,000 showed up in many different ways. I was so shocked that I started telling my friends about it. Before I knew it hundreds of people in this town had wads of cash showing up in their lives. Every day I was receiving bouquets of flowers and phone calls of gratitude for the empowerment that I was facilitating. We were all having so much fun, and people were willing to step up and empower those around them. I often recall that time of empowering others and it still brings me immense joy. Empowerment is one of the main elements that makes up my platform.

Your personal platform is going to be different from mine and those of other people. It should be about living the way you would like to live, not the way that you are supposed to, or how others want you to. If you could see what your platform was, then you couldn't make yourself wrong ever again. Wherever you see yourself as wrong, it's a place where you are denying your platform. When you eliminate the elements of your platform, you are choosing against you and limiting you. Your platform should be about living the way you would like to live.

If you will start to get the energy of the platform of your life and start basking in that energy and that possibility, it can create an energy of ease from which everything starts to flow. It becomes fun to be alive, because you are starting to function from the energy of you.

When you are making choices, if you ask, "Will this expand my agenda or contract my agenda?" you'll know what to choose. Would you be willing to look at what is going to expand or contract your agenda in life?

Everything that you desire in life is based on your platform. Whatever your personal agenda is, that's part of your platform, which is based on what being you is. Even if you don't know what your platform is, when you function from it, what becomes relevant is only that which expands your agenda. With a platform, you always have a place from which to create something greater. It is not about finding what your platform is. It is about recognizing that somewhere you have one.

What choices can you make that will expand your agenda and create more life and living? When you make a choice and it contracts your agenda and your platform, your life gets smaller. Whatever your platform is, that's irrelevant. Your platform is the place from which you build the agenda called "creating your life." Your agenda is what you as an infinite being would like to be, do, have, create and generate. When you ask the question, you will feel a sense of lightness or contraction, and the lightness is what you want to go for, whether it makes sense to you or not.

Your platform is you and your agenda is everything you would like to be and do.

Questions to Empower You

- What are the elements of my platform?
- Am I using my platform for me or against me?
- Does this choice expand my agenda?
- What do I desire to create and generate?

What if?

- What if you created your life based on your platform?
- What if creating your life is you being you?

Generative life has no target, it has no goal and it has no purpose. Goals, plans, purposes and mission statements are contextual reality. Are you willing to receive the speed with which something can come to you? Are you willing to be the joy of it?

~ Gary Douglas

The platform opens the door for you to have anything and everything in your life, not just one line you have to take or one thing you have to do. It's not a target and it's not a goal. It's a platform off of which every missile of your reality can be shot.

~ Gary Douglas

CHAPTER THIRTEEN

What Can I Add to My Life?

What else can I add to my life that would bring me more money that would give me more joy that would give me more of me? What would your life be like if you lived as this question?

If you don't have enough going on in your life, you may start creating lots of problems. What would you really like to create? Are you eliminating things from your life so you can get your life under control? Do you like to create from chaos? Notice when you have too much to do, you're happiest.

This is very true for me. At the moment I am writing three books, creating classes worldwide, writing workshops, designing websites and asking, "What else can I add to my life and living?" It is chaotic and I love it. People are demanding of me every day for the pieces that they require to be the contribution to my projects. Do I have a sense of pressure? Yes, and I don't let it get to me, I just stay in the question of what is required and I follow the energy.

What if it isn't about simplifying your life? What if you added things to your life, not removed things from it? Do you ever notice that when you are working on something you enjoy, you forget to eat? You have plenty of energy, you are totally present, you are happy beyond your wildest dreams.

To generate your life, you must generate outside of this reality, not generate inside this reality, otherwise all you can do is align and agree with other people's point of view.

Your life can sit outside this reality and does not have to be a part of it. To have your life does not require anyone else to agree with any point of view that you have or any awareness you have. If you wish to have total awareness then what you must seek is your life, not a reality. There is no reality that is real except when two or more people make it so.

Beyond this reality, you generate from space. Generating from and as space, you continually generate from more space and you don't have to go back into the suffering you used to call your life. You just keep asking "What else is possible?"

Do you spend a lot of your time looking to the past as a reference point as though there must be some truth or reality to it? The past is the only way you can perpetuate the limitations you currently have into the future. If you gave up all your past, then you'd have to start living your life today and you'd have nothing to talk about—which is why you keep the past in existence. As long as you have a good victim story then you have a way to keep creating relationship with people.

The more I destroy my past reference points, the more I am out of the limitations of what I have created and projecting them into my future. The funny thing is, I can now be with people and have nothing to talk about. I am very happy to be in silence when I am with people. I use my past stories during classes and in my books as a way to empower people to see how they are using their past reference points as limitations to destroy themselves and their future. I now see them for what they are, just stories that I have used in the past to keep me in the victim role and stuck in this reality. Creating a reality is all the busyness of doing things for other people, which I have been really good at. For me that has always created a sense of resentment. Now instead of doing that, I look at a time when I was really joyful in what I was doing and I had no sense of giving up any part of me in order to be happy and I choose from that energy.

You can't generate your life from the past, from the obligations or the promises.

What if promises were only good for this moment?

Is Motivation Destroying You?

Are you using a menu of motivating factors? What if the only real motivation is choice? When you create motivation to create your life, you're not actually generating your life. All you're doing is creating the pressure cooker that forces you into doing things. How many problems have you created in your life to force you into getting conscious and more aware? Have you created no money, bad relationships, bad health or pain in your body or life to force you to choose more awareness? Would you be willing to acknowledge that you created that so you'd get conscious?

What if you never made a wrong choice? How much of what you have chosen in the past was designed to get you here today, so you would actually choose for you, as you, as consciousness?

I can now acknowledge that most of my life I have been really good at getting money and really good at getting rid of money. When Gary was facilitating me in a class one day around money, he got me to look at this. When I acknowledged it I then knew that I could change it. I have always been great at giving money away, not being present and aware of what people could receive, and often times I ended up with a knife in my back because they couldn't receive it. I can now allow myself to have money, and the universe responds by flowing so much more to me.

How much of your life have you lived based on the motivation of "I don't have any money" or, the motivation of "I have got to do this to maintain my relationship" or, the motivation of "I need to create a life like everybody else."

What if you didn't have motivation as a source for generation any more, what if it were choice? This is very different to what we have been told about creating in this reality.

How much of your life do you spend doing things you don't actually like?

How much of your life is spent fulfilling someone else's needs, wants and desires; society's needs, wants and desires and the obligations of society or what everybody else tells you is the source of life?

The majority of the world has no motivation for life. How many people are just avoiding death as though that's having a life?

If you get to where you feel like a bit of a couch potato with no motivation, what's left for you to create a life with? What if it is time for new choices and you being you? Are you willing to step into that? Or are you in resistance to life?

If you are truly willing to generate a life, you have to be willing to be, do, have, create or generate anything and everything. A "life" is the willingness to be or do anything you have to do or be in order to generate what you would like to have in your life.

What Is Required to Generate a Life?

You want the life you want to show up for you, but are you willing to do what it takes to get it? Do you expect things to show up for you because you have asked? "Ask and you shall receive" has become a limitation. You have to be willing to do whatever it takes.

Are you willing to use all the tools in your tool box?

If you lived as a question you would start generating the life you want. You have to be willing to be or do whatever you have to be or do to get what you want.

Is money your motivation? Is that great enough to be worth going after aggressively? Instead, if you go after awareness and consciousness (perceiving, knowing, being and receiving) and you are willing to be, do, have, create or generate *anything* to get there, you will get what you want. You have to have that kind of aggression.

See what you want and go for it as aggressively as possible.

Allowance is knowing you're hitting your head up against a brick wall here and going, "Ok, that isn't working…what else can I do? What can I do different?" If you go after something and nothing happens, don't say, "I will make it happen.". That's hitting your head up against a brick wall assuming if you hit it hard enough you will get through. Instead ask, "What can I do different here? Why am I hitting my head against the wall when there's an open door over there? I'll go through the open door instead!"

Know what's right for you and go for it, whether anyone else agrees with it or not.

I just had a phone call with my daughter and she was asking me how I was going with the book. I said that I was looking at pressing the send button to the publisher tonight. As I said those words, tears of joy sprang to my eyes, as I considered what I have been creating.

When I was at school English was never an easy language for me. As a matter of fact, in high school I got higher grades for French and German than I ever did for English. So the prospect of ever writing a book just didn't exist in my world until two years ago. In realizing how much these tool and techniques have created so much change for me and my clients, I truly desired to contribute to getting them out into the world, whilst not being vested in the outcome of what that looked like.

As I had the awareness of what I desired to create, the idea of writing a book after my teleclass series seemed like the natural next step. I have been aware of the moments when I felt like I was hitting my head on a brick wall, so it was in those moments I went to question and walked away from the computer. However, it has been, This is what I'm doing; this is where I'm going". I have been working on it for two years—and I don't have a point of view about that.

It was always my target to get it published and to do whatever it takes. Researching the information for this book has been incredibly empowering for me and I have received this information on a new level of awareness.

What would it take for the people who are looking for this information to find this book? Now I am getting ready for the next project and I will aggressively pursue that, as that's the determination that I choose to go after what I wish to have as my life; to be the leader in my life. I will not give up on where I am going. I will be persistent and continue to go after what I know. to be true for me.

It can be uncomfortable to pursue what you know and to be aggressive. Aggressive presence is never being less in order to make somebody else be more. Aggressive presence means you are there being you and you won't change for somebody else's point of view. When you are aggressively present, you stand up and you are just there being you. When you do aggression, you are the catalyst for what creates a different possibility. It allows you to be a gift that inspires others. With aggression, you don't back down from what you know. You're aware of what you're aware of, and you don't apologize for it. If you are aggressively present, you can be arrogant, you can be kind, you can be caring and you can be everything. If you're not aggressively present as you, then you always have to give you up to be of service to someone else. You want to be aggressively present so that you are a source to be reckoned with and a force that cannot be stopped. If you use judgement as greater than you, you are eliminating aggressive presence in favour of other people's points of view.

Just keep on demanding more of you "No matter what it takes, I will be and do and generate whatever it takes to get this or have this." You have to demand it of yourself! Sometimes it means doing the dirty work. You have to be willing to deal with everything- the good, the bad and the ugly.

What goes along with aggressive presence is aggressive kindness. Aggressive kindness is never force. It's a presence.

You are the gift that people desire.

Aggressive kindness is also where you actually take care of you.

Aggressive kindness can be: *"I'm sorry. This doesn't work for me."*

You've got to be willing to have the level of presence which imposes your awareness on people to the degree that they can't choose what is going to destroy them.

Aggressive kindness invites them not to destroy themselves.

Questions to Empower You

- Is this part of my platform?
- Will this expand my agenda?
- What else can I add to my life that would bring me more money that would give me more joy that would give me more of me?
- What can I do differently?
- What else would I like to add to my life that would generate more consciousness, more possibilities and generate a different world?

What if?

- What if adding to your life brings you more fun, joy and money?
- What if life was meant to be easy and not hard?
- What if it isn't about simplifying your life?
- What if promises were only good for this moment?
- What if the only real motivation is choice?

- What if you didn't have motivation as a source for generation any more, what if it were choice?

- What if it is time for new choices and you being you?

You want to create from life—changing, reality—changing choices. When you do that, you open the door to everything that is possible. If you really want to create the life you'd like to have, you're going to have to create from the big choices, not the little choices.

~ Gary Douglas

CHAPTER FOURTEEN

Being a Conscious Leader

Conscious leadership is the willingness to know where you're going whether anybody else goes along or not and you're still going to go.

It is you knowing that you are going where you have to go, not thinking or expecting that other people need to go where you go.

If you have the courage to know where you are going, to know where you want to be, to know what you want to do—whether anybody else goes along or not—you will never give you away. You will always choose that which you know creates space. You will do that which is being, that which joy is. You will do that which you perceive as expansive and thus you will receive the intensity of the judgement, the wondrousness, the beauty and everything else with total ease. But, unless you are willing to be a leader, it won't happen.

What is the value of never having the courage to be different and be a leader?

If you would like to be a leader in your own life, you might ask, "What does consciousness require of me?" When a door opens, you'll know that's where you have to go. It's about learning to allow the universe to show you where to go, rather than coming to conclusion.

Are you living by other people's needs, wants and desires of you? Would you be willing to step into the courage that is you?

Courage is the ability to be different and to have no point of view about your difference; to be courage, regardless of what anybody and their points of view are, regardless of the circumstances. You know where you have to go and you will go regardless what anyone else thinks. You go without judgement.

A person who is a true leader knows what is right for them, regardless of whether anybody else gets it or not. Being the leader of your own life requires you to be you.

Leading is being aware and recognizing that you are the generator for everything in your life.

A leader never knows where they are going. They just go. If people follow them, then they're the leader. If nobody follows them, then they're still the leader. A true leader only has to ask a question and invite you to the party. If you're a leader, you can't have a point of view. You just know that you're on your way. When you're doing soft and seductive, you're doing leadership. When you're truly being a leader, you don't come across as intense.

When you're doing control and not-leader, you come across as intense, because you are not willing to receive what anyone is willing to gift to you. If somebody cares for you intensely, you have to give up control and receive. Having somebody care for you requires for you to be the leader. If they truly care for you, they will not enjoy you beating them away. You will bash them away so you can prove that they do not really care.

If you are willing to be a leader, then you don't have to constantly micro-manage your life and obsessively do everything all by yourself so you can control everything. If you're the leader, you don't have to do everything, and you can do everything. You don't have to control everything, and you can allow it to lead you into a different possibility in life. You need no one and you can receive everyone.

What if being the ultimate leader is just being and doing whatever you want whenever you want to do it? That just means that nobody can control you. You can't control or lead by example. If you're a real leader, you don't care if somebody is following you. If you are truly a leader, you can receive from everybody. You take the part that works for you and leave the part that doesn't.

When you're not willing to be the leader, you must of necessity find the wrongness of you. What if you generated your life instead of this one? You have to be willing to be never right, never wrong and always aware. Some of you will be willing to be the leader, and some won't, but you will never be a follower. You have to be willing to be a follower or else you will not be able to follow your awareness.

The Joy of Being You

Have you been running your life on automatic pilot? Has it been an accumulation of the answers of what you think you got right, that you keep doing and perpetrating over and over and over and over again. Is that enough for you?

On the other hand, there is this thing called "being," where you wake up and ask, "What would be fun and rewarding for me today? What would bring me joy to do today? What would be more fun to do today than anything else I can do?"

Then whatever it takes you go and do it!

You may have to go to your job, so ask, "What would be fun to do today at my job? What part of this would be joyful for me today?" Then go and do it. You would be amazed that when you actually add this weird little thing called "joy" to your life, how much easier your life gets. It gets more fun, and it gets more space, and then money shows up and you don't even know why. People are giving you money, and you look at your bank account and go, "Wow, money, okay! How does it get any better than this?" That is very joyful.

Would it be joyful for you to receive money in your bank account? Are you willing to let some joy into your life to have that joyful experience? What if you lived life for the fun of it? What if a generative life was a life that's dedicated to how joyful your life can truly be?

Your whole life should be about doing it for fun. What if you did everything in your life for the fun of it? How much of your work are you doing because it is fun? How much of it are you doing because you are obligated to do it? How much of it are you doing because you need the money? How much of it are you doing because you have to pay the bills?

Doing What You Love

If you start doing something you love, your whole energy will be working for you; your business will expand and everything will open up. As you start to put more energy into generating your life, everything else in your life expands by osmosis because that energy of generating more in your life generates more and you will have more of you in your life.

When you are too busy to do what you love, everything contracts. Don't ever make it so you are too busy to do what gives you joy. Have you made your life just work? Would you be willing to do what generates your life? If you go for a run, go to the movies or ride a horse or anything that is fun, then that generative energy contributes to your life. You often come back from that run or ride with a great idea for your business. Why? Because you are no longer focused on something; you are receiving and that opens the doors to awareness. Your life is about the joy of it. Are you trying to have a "successful" life? There is judgement in having a "successful" life.

One of the things that I love to do is cook. And I particularly love to cook for my family and friends. For instance, I enjoyed preparing for a family dinner when my son and his new wife came to visit from

Hong Kong. For many people this would be harrowing as when I cook I really cook and I love serving up to ten dishes. In the morning I worked on the menu and then prepared the grocery list. Off I headed to the grocery store to get all the goodies for the big cook up. The energy of contribution from what I had done already towards the meal preparation inspired me to write more on this book in the afternoon. Even the shopping for the food was fun for me, carefully selecting the food that would be nourishing for my family and I.

What do you love to do that is fun and joyful? What if being the energy of that 24/7 expands your life and living?

If I show up for the fun of it, the money flows. Are you willing to work half as hard as everybody else and make twice the amount of money? That is the way to live your life as an adventure—with the question, "I wonder what this will be like?" What if you never do anything that you don't want to do?

I have spent a large part of my life doing things that I didn't want to do, so now if I don't want to do something, I simply don't do it. Once it stops being fun and I know that I am not having fun anymore I move on. There is no fun in suffering. Ease, joy and glory is not pain, suffering and gory. Would you be willing to get crystal clear about that? Asking this question will bring you so much awareness: "What would it take for me to have a life of total ease, joy and glory?"

Have you become serious or has your life always been serious? How much laughter is there in your life? How much joy is there? Or are there just lots of judgements? What if you could walk through this world and be the awareness that judgement wasn't a necessity?

You have to see the humour of things. People fighting for money are simply amusing. They are fighting over money to prove that they are not losing. You have made your money serious. How much money are you going to have to have for it to be a laughing matter for you? How much money would you have to have so you could just mess with people for the fun of it? Would you be willing to laugh at yourself?

Questions to Empower You

- What is the value of never having the courage to be different and be a leader?
- What would it take to be the leader of my own life?
- What if being the ultimate leader is just being and doing whatever I want whenever I want to do it?

What if?

- What if being conscious is the experience of expanding our awareness beyond its current limitations?
- What if being kind, caring and not judging, not making yourself or others wrong, is you being a great gift?

You have got to get that the gift you have is the ability to perceive when most people are sitting in judgement, sitting in discomfort. The majority of the world is not comfortable, in case you hadn't noticed. Most people are not happy. Most people are not looking for fun.

~ Gary Douglas

CHAPTER FIFTEEN

Choosing Happiness or Unhappiness

What if happiness or unhappiness is just a choice? Do you get the sense that the majority of the world likes unhappiness? All kinds of people choose unhappiness. People love and are addicted to trauma and drama, upset and intrigue. Are you aware that the three primary emotions that run this earth are anger, grief and sadness? Most people don't want you to be happy, they want you to be like them, which is unhappy. How many people attend church on a Sunday and then are mean, unkind and unhappy for the rest of the week? For what reason would they choose that?

Do you have the point of view that unhappiness is more real than happiness because more people are unhappy than are happy? We are trained to be unhappy. People will say to you, "Oh you poor thing," when you are unhappy. If you are happy they say, "What drug are you on?" True happiness is about the peace and joy that is possible. Unhappiness is a manufactured emotional state of not being that justifies a whole lot of misery. You can't actually be unhappy unless you work at it.

If peace and joy were the operative states on this planet, would we have jails, war, hospitals, therapists or governments? How many of these systems have been put in place to keep unhappiness in existence? Without unhappiness, the world would fall apart. Unhappiness is the kingpin for holding the world together as it currently is. The more you laugh, the more it heals the earth. If you actually had to be happy, then you would transmute all the suffering on planet earth into total joy and then you would have nothing to do. There would be no way of holding society in the jail it's currently in.

What if depression is a choice people make because they want to be unhappy? If you are unhappy enough, then your depression allows you to be given drugs, or allows you to go to therapy. It also allows you to go to church and pray; it allows you to do what is considered right in this reality. It makes it possible for you to not have to work.

Some years ago I was contracted to work with long term unemployed people to get them back into the workforce. A large majority of them were on anti-depressants. This, of course, gave them the "out" for getting a job. After working with them for a few days the majority of them started to see that they were totally bored with their lives and unhappy. They weren't creating their lives of choice, and they had no clue as to what that really was. Many were from families who had generations of un-employment and depression. I would ask them, "Who does this depression belong to?" "Is it your depression?" Most of them would laugh and say no, it isn't mine.

Do you know that you are far more psychic than you ever give yourself credit for? You are like the psychic "Sponge Bob" of the universe. You are aware. You think that if a thought, feeling or emotion fits in your reality, it must be yours. It's never yours. When you get that, you will finally have total freedom.

What if spending three days asking: "Who does this belong to?" for every thought, feeling and emotion you have gave you total freedom? Three days of asking, "Who does this belong to?" will set you free of all the thoughts, feelings and emotions other people have. It will be the most work you have ever done in your life. For every thought, feeling and emotion you have, ask this question. If it lightens up at all, just return it to sender. It's not yours. (When something makes you feel light, that is because it is true for you. When something is heavy that is because it is a lie for you).

The third day, about halfway through the day, all of a sudden, you'll have no thoughts in your head, and you'll become a walking, talking meditation.

Meditation for me was always interesting. Just prior to studying Naturopathy I had chronic fatigue. I knew that I had to make some new choices, so meditation was something that I added to my life. I would sit quietly, and as fast as the thoughts moved through, my head would fill with many more. Of course it was so easy to make me wrong again and judge myself that I couldn't even meditate when everyone else could. When I came to Access Consciousness® and learned this tool, so much changed in my life. I finally realised that none of the thoughts, feelings and emotions were mine. The peace that I now have in my world is astounding as finally I am free of the "monkey mind."

What if all thoughts, feelings and emotions are your justification system for everything in your life? What are you going to share with people when you are happy? You have no thoughts, feelings and emotions to share, because nobody wants those. If you were being telepathic and not having a thought and not trying to share your limited points of view with one another, you would be joyful all the time.

Are you looking for happiness outside of you? You have to create happiness in yourself in order to have somebody in your life who can be equally as happy as you are. Can anybody or anything make you happy? Why would you give anyone or anything outside of you the power to make you happy or sad, rather than you being the source of happiness? "I am happy when I do these things," is different from, "These things make me happy." Then if they disappear or can't be around, you have no happiness. What would you like to build your life from?

Creating Happiness with Joy, Peace and Possibility

What if the greatest gift that you have, that you could give to the world more than anything else, is total consciousness? If you chose to be and see the gift of you, no matter what occurred, if you made that your target in life, you would do more for the planet than anyone else. You would inspire and invite people to be willing to be more of them. Would you be willing to contribute to the whole world and have the whole world contribute to you?

If you don't look at the bigger picture, you can't be all of you. If you won't be that gift, you can't actually change what's happening on planet earth. You have to be the all of you in order to instigate the quantum entanglements that will create a shift in reality. The earth has an amazing capacity to rejuvenate itself, but you have to be in allowance of what the earth chooses also. If enough of us were willing to be the gift of who we be, we could change the entire earth.

Are you still looking for what to do? What if there is no "how" to be? What if there is only, "What would I like to choose in this moment? What would be joyful? What would be fun? What would bring huge amounts of money that I would totally enjoy doing right now?"

Would you like to make a miraculous transition, taking the old you and turning into a new you? Are you willing to not know who you are for a while? Are you ready to step into something greater? Please know that it never shows up how you think it will, so please don't conclude what it will be or look like, that one I know from my own life. But in order to go from where you are and who you are, and who you've decided you are not—to get to who you actually are, is going to require some period of where you have no clue who you are.

You have to be willing to have no clue. You have to be willing to wake up and ask, "Who am I today and what grand and glorious adventures and true magic am I going to have?" which means you have to continually generate your life.

If you are not willing to have a life without reference points, if you're not willing to walk around and have no clue who you are all the time, then you are being run by this reality. You're saying you'd rather have contextual reality than have the generation of your life.

This is the necessity of being in the question and living as the question. When you wake up in the morning, ask, "Who am I today?" Because then and only then are you actually generating your life.

If you are going to generate your life as a phenomenon, it will be something other than that which has existed here before. Does it make sense to you that it is not cognitive? This reality would tell you "the known" is what you want and that is all you should want. That if you don't know it, it is going to be bad for you. That if you haven't seen it before and haven't already defined it, it is going to be bad for you. Is that true, or is that an implanted point of view?

Living Life as a Celebration

Would you be willing to live your life as a celebration? Are there any reasons as to why you would want to live your life from the trauma and drama, upset and intrigue? What if, when you or your friends got fired or ended a relationship you would go out, buy great champagne, and celebrate? Congratulations, what if this is actually the best day of your life? What if this is the beginning of a whole new life for you? What else can you create and add to your life and living? Let's now toast to the future, not the past.

Often when I get together with my daughter and I bring out the great champagne, she asks me how come we are drinking this great stuff? For me now, it is about living in the moment. "If this is the last moment of my life, what would I choose?" Life is too short to not drink delicious champagne!

When I reflect over the years of my life, one thing that I know for sure is that as one door closes another opens that always opens to far greater possibilities. At the time if you are uncomfortable with the changes, your discomfort may just be two seconds before you get you.

I know that I am happiest when I am creating and participating in life. Many years ago when I was participating on a "Designing Your Life" programme, we were asked to write our Eulogy. "What would I want to be remembered as and what would I want my headstone to say?" I have always remembered that process, and when I find myself going down the rabbit hole of wrongness, I recall what I wrote on those pages. I am now willing to look at what can be—not what should be. A different reality can occur when I look at what can be.

I am so grateful for what people do for me. I realise I could be gone tomorrow.

It is time to acknowledge people, always be kind, and not take things personally. It's time to ask questions and change the energy instead of being miserable and unhappy. As a little kid I always knew that there was so much more to life. Before too long I could only see finite possibilities and limitations. Everything had to be done the way that everyone else did it. What if what I knew was possible as a kid actually is possible?

There *is* a different way. There *is* a different possibility. There is this energy, space and consciousness that is a possibility for the generation of your life. *Are you ready to choose it?*

Now that we have looked at what is required, would you indulge in anything and refine your indulgence?

Questions to Empower You

- What would I like to build my life from?

- What can I do? Where can I be that would change something and make this easier for the planet?

- What would I like to choose in this moment?

- What would be joyful?

- What would be fun?

- What would bring huge amounts of money that I would totally enjoy doing right now?

- Who am I today and what grand and glorious adventures am I going to have?

- What would it take for me to have a life of total ease, joy and glory?

- What else can you create and add to your life and living?

What if?

- What if happiness is just a choice?

- What if your life didn't get better by chance, it got better by choice?

- What if the only thing that you resist is the fullest expression of you?

- What if what I knew was possible as a kid actually is?

- What if this is the best day of your life?

- What if this is the beginning of a whole new life for you?

Would you indulge in anything and refine your indulgence? Indulgence done from refinement cannot be wrong! When you are willing to live your life from a hedonistic pleasure place, your life begins to work in ways it never has before, because you are living for the joy of it, not for what you have to accomplish, what you have to do, or for any life purposes.

~ Gary Douglas

About the Author

Margaret Braunack has over 25 years of experience in the fields of health, personal and professional development in various roles, including management, sales, mentoring, coaching, training and development. She also has had over twenty years in the Creative Arts, from designing and making theatre, opera and ballet costumes to bridal and evening wear and high-end fashion. During this time she created many businesses.

She has worked and trained with some of the world's leading organizations, mentors and coaches and she has gained the knowledge and techniques to truly know how to facilitate anyone to instant success.

She is a Natural Therapist, bodyworker, an internationally recognized trainer in Neuro Linguistic Programming (NLP), as well as a National Values Trainer, certified Master Time Line Therapist, a certified Master Hypnotherapist, mentor, coach, a dynamic international keynote speaker and seminar presenter and a licensed Facilitator of Access Consciousness®—Empowering People to Know that they Know.

She covers a wide range of seminar and workshop topics and specializes in Leadership, Money & Business, Employment Training, Conscious Relationships with Children, Finding You and Your

Voice in Your Relationships, and Sex & Relationships. She is currently working on a new seminar series based on this book.

Her seminars, presentations, workshops and private sessions are dynamic, fun, light, humorous and life-changing.

She has worked with adults and children who have been labelled as ADD, ADHD and Autism with amazing results, and also facilitates students of all ages to great improvement with their studies. She taught a hands-on body process called "The BARS" to the inmates of a Brisbane prison. This programme was affectionately called "BARS behind Bars."

Margaret is willing to assist you in developing greater possibilities and provide you with the tools and techniques that will change you forever. Are you ready to change any area of your life that is not working for you? Whether it is your physical health and body, mental, emotional or spiritual well-being, Margaret can gift you with more. What else is truly possible for you, your body and your life?

For more information about Margaret Braunack, go to www.margaretbraunack.com.

Testimonial

"To me Margaret Braunack personifies hedonism, opulence, decadence and orgasmic living.

Margaret will tell you herself she comes from humble beginnings and was not born into wealth and yet she has such ease and comfort with luxury and encourages all of us to participate in the joy of hedonism.

Having participated in Margaret's courses her tele-call series, and the changes that have shown up in my world, now all I can ask is, "Why did I wait so long?"

Thanks to Margaret's inspiration I now own pearls, gold, diamonds, silver and I have drunk Verve Clicquot champagne, eaten exquisite foods, bought clothes that caress my body with their loveliness. I now drink out of bone china cups, sleep on delicious sheets and have furnishings that I adore. I truly never considered this was available to me because of the programming and points of view I had bought into and made real in my world. Clearing these points of view with Margaret enabled me to change my world. I use her guiding questions every day and it's amazing the possibilities that show up for me to consider.

Being a hedonist does not have to cost masses of money...it's being aware of glory all around us and being willing to receive it all into you and your world. Once you begin to receive it all, it's so wonderful! Thank you Margaret, I adore you."

~ Christine, Melbourne Australia

Other Access Consciousness® Books

Divorceless Relationships
By Gary M. Douglas

Most of us spend a lot of time divorcing parts and pieces of ourselves in order to care for someone else. For example, you like to go jogging but instead of jogging, you spend that time with your partner to show him or her that you really care. "I love you so much that I would give up this thing that is valuable to me so I can be with you." This is one of the ways you divorce you to create an intimate relationship. How often does divorcing you really work in the long run?

Being You, Changing the World
By Dr. Dain Heer

Have you always known that something COMPLETELY DIFFERENT is possible? What if you had a handbook for infinite possibilities and dynamic change to guide you? With tools and processes that actually worked and invited you to a completely different way of being? For you? And the world?

Would You Teach a Fish to Climb a Tree?
By Anne Maxwell, Gary M. Douglas, and Dr. Dain Heer

A Different Take on Kids with ADD, ADHD, OCD and Autism. People tend to function from the point of view that there is something wrong with these children because they don't learn the way the rest of us do. The reality is that they pick things up in a totally different manner. This book takes a look at that and so much more!

Pragmatic Psychology:
Practical Tools For Being Crazy Happy
By Susanna Mittermaier

Everyone has at least one "crazy" person in their life, right (even if it's ourselves!)? And there are a lot of labels and diagnoses out there—depression, anxiety, ADD, ADHD, bi-polar, schizophrenia... What if there was a different possibility with mental illness—and what if change and happiness were a totally available reality? Susanna is a clinical psychologist with an amazing capacity to facilitate what this reality often defines as crazy from a totally different point of view—one of possibility and ease.

Right Recovery for You
By Marilyn Bradford

No matter what your addiction is, or how long you have had it *Right Recovery For You* can help you change it. This is a totally new approach to addiction that you won't find anywhere else. Developed by Marilyn Bradford and utilizing information and process for change from Access Consciousness® founder Gary Douglas, you can have a totally different possibility for ending your addiction for good, or getting it to something that works for you.